MW00946114

Marriage, Money and Romance

God's Plan for You

by
Donny Ingram

authorHOUSE™

1663 LIBERTY DRIVE, SUITE 200
BLOOMINGTON, INDIANA 47403
(800) 839-8640
WWW.AUTHORHOUSE.COM

First published by AuthorHouse 04/07/05

ISBN: 1-4208-4147-5 (sc)

Library of Congress Control Number: 2005903216

Printed in the United States of America
Bloomington, Indiana

This book is printed on acid-free paper.

Cover Design by Matt Owens
mowens@mcwatersassociates.com

Cover Photo by Rick Poon
rkpoon@excite.com

Proof reading by Marilyn Stith,
Amber Ingram and Carolyn Ford
Oneonta, Alabama

Dedication

I dedicate this book to my lovely wife, Charlotte and our three sons, Brad, Josh and Tyler. Without them I would never have understood or experienced such a wonderful and beautiful life as a husband, father and now a grandfather. Charlotte and I have been married over thirty years and if more wives loved their husbands as she loves me, fewer men would be enticed to look over the fence for something more. Brad and Josh are out of the nest and raising their own families and fulfilling God's purpose for their lives. Tyler is now in college equipping himself for the future and very excited about the possibilities. I feel secure in their love and extremely blessed to have such a dedicated, level-headed, God-fearing wife and sons who are committed to serving God with their talents and abilities.

I also want to dedicate this to my father and mother, Billy Joe and Maxine Ingram. Even though my father has gone on to heaven, the knowledge and example he gave me of how to treat a wife and raise children has contributed immensely to my success as a husband and father. My mom has always been a strong tower and the mother that every child longs to have. Their love for each other and the way they expressed love instilled in me the desire to seek the same for myself.

Acknowledgments

First and foremost I must acknowledge the one who makes it all possible, our Lord and Savior Jesus Christ. Without him I could do nothing.

I'm also extremely indebted to a host of professionals who have greatly influenced my life through personal testimonies, books, tapes and seminars. Among them are people like Gary Chapman, Gary Smalley, Edwin Louis Cole, Myles Munroe, Gene A. Getz, Zig Ziglar, Charles Capps, Randy and Susan Eubanks, Frankie and Laura Powell, Norman Vincent Peale, Perry Stone, John Maxwell, Stu Weber and Al Taylor. Along with them are the many couples and close friends that have shared their lives with me over the past thirty plus years. This book is a tribute to their inspiration, revelation and success in reaching and enriching lives.

Forward

Donny Ingram has written an outstanding guidebook for the home in the 21st Century. His experience in life and family, his dedication to the relationships he holds dear, his value of people and his commitment to Christ is found in the pages of this book.

He has used wit, wisdom and the Word of God to make successful family, solid finances, and a great future not only applicable, but easily available to every person who reads his message. Donny has intertwined his personal openness with the knowledge of many great authors and teachers and most importantly the principles found in the oldest book of wisdom, the Bible. I recommend "Marriage, Money and Romance" to all those not yet married, newly married, and those married for a long time. Donny has in actuality given us a portrayal of how to live in such a way that the generations who follow us will experience the blessings of that which we pass on.

Because I know him personally, I see the evidence of this book in the life of his wife, children and his grandchildren. If you follow his roadmap, it will lead to a life worth living filled with the blessings of eternal truths that will not fail.

God bless you Donny for loving your family enough, the Body of Christ as much, and Jesus even more, to take the time and effort to make these principles available to us.

I count you as a personal friend.

Your Fellow Laborer,
Frankie Powell

Contents

Introduction

Many years ago I was told that God gave me two ends, one to think with and one to sit on, and my success in life would be determined by which one I used the most. While I found this to be humorous it made me realize an incredible truth. Everything in life centers on decisions. In fact I believe there are three things that will determine where you go and how successful you are in life. Number one are the people you meet, number two are the books you read and number three are the decisions you make. The first two speak for themselves but as humans we are the only creatures on earth given the ability to make decisions. All other creatures are born with what is known as "instinct." This instinct is what causes bears to hibernate, geese to fly south in the winter, or salmon to swim upstream. These creatures can't even question their actions because it's built into them. But you and I as humans are given the power to create our own future. And we do exactly that. Every day we put into place actions and ideas that will shape and form our future.

For some, these actions and ideas lead them to a life filled with achievements, rewards, joy, health, and wealth. For others it tends to lead to a life of ups and downs, never really being able to reach their full potential or enjoy every day. And for a great number of people it leads to a life of depression, oppression, anger, poverty, sickness, divorce, and sometimes an early death.

I want you to realize that success or failure as a husband, wife, father, or mother is not a matter of luck. It's not a matter of circumstance, fate, the breaks, who you know or any other myth or cliché which some tend to use for an excuse. It is a matter of following a common sense set of guidelines and principles anyone can follow. When we follow the guidelines and apply the principles, we can create the moments in life that matter the most. We can become the persons God designed us to be, do the things that create love, joy, and happiness in ourselves and others. We can have all that God planned for us in this life. But, in order to achieve these goals we must follow His guidelines which are documented in the best selling book of all time -- The Bible. While many argue over religion, denominational views, and personal beliefs, the guidelines set by God will work for anyone and everyone who chooses to believe and follow His principles.

In the Bible we find that the first institution God founded was the family. In fact He established three vital institutions — family (home), church, and government. The family was God's first because it is the basis for everything else. Abraham Lincoln said, "The strength of a nation lies in the homes of its people." In other words, he's saying that the state of our nation can be accredited to the condition of our marriages, families and homes. I believe the family is the most important single factor in the molding of a human being. It either prepares us to reach for God's ultimate destiny and fulfillment, or it prevents us from achieving His original purpose for our life.

The Bible tells us that man was incomplete by himself. Most everyone who has attended vacation bible school or Sunday school is familiar with the story in Genesis chapter 2 where Adam named the animals that came before him. The passage of scripture concludes with the words *"...but for Adam there was not found a helper comparable to him."* Then we read the beautiful story of God's special provision, *"He took one of his ribs, and closed up the flesh in its place. Then the rib which the Lord God had taken from man He made into a woman, and He brought her to the man."* Many believe this was the first wedding and God performed the first marriage ceremony. From then until now no other factor in human life has been more significant than the marriage relationship and the family.

The family, according to Genesis chapter 2 verses 18-25, is to provide a haven for its members, a place where we prepare for entering society, a place where we begin to recognize and understand our purpose in life: how to serve God, and serve others. Today with half of all marriages ending in divorce we have problems that are passed from generation to generation. Problems like children having to live outside the home, many homes dealing with abuse, neglect or something even worse. I believe its time we go back and understand what God intended for marriage and learn how we can start living the successful, happy and healthy, purposeful life He intended for us to live.

In the following pages I want to draw your attention to the marriage relationship and very briefly look at the role of a wife, husband, parent, and servant. The principles in this book are just a few to help you understand the basics of what God has outlined for marriage.

My hope and prayer is that more couples will begin to recognize and identify their responsibility and become the persons and mates God intended for them to be. I want more people to fulfill the purpose God has for them and avoid many of the pitfalls in life. I want you to begin to do the things that matter the most in life, and receive all the promises of God physically, socially, spiritually and financially.

1

Lord,
I want to
be Married

The first explanation of the man-woman relationship is found in the first book of the Bible - Genesis chapter 2 verse 24, *"Therefore a man shall leave his father and mother and be joined to his wife, and they shall become one flesh."* Marriage is every young lady's dream, every man's desire and God's plan for a man and woman.

I remember how much I wanted to be married when I was a young boy. I remember asking God to allow my future wife and me to have sons. I wanted to be married so bad that I proposed to several young women before receiving a yes from the woman God had planned for me. And today I thank God that he didn't allow marriage to happen until I found Charlotte.

Our oldest son, Brad, had the same desire to be married as I. From the ninth grade he began looking for a potential wife. I'm pleased to say he found the beautiful godly woman that God prepared for him, and they're happily married and have two great children. In fact, our second son, Josh, found the love of his life almost two years ago and they're enjoying the wonderful journey of marriage also. That desire to leave parents and join to another person is planted inside us by God for His purposes.

Every young man and woman, at a magic age, begins to long for someone to share their life with. When we think we've found that special someone there is something inside we call the "in-love" sensation that greatly influences our ability to see clearly and make decisions wisely. This in-love sensation blinds us to many issues that should be discussed and ironed out before getting too far into the relationship. Now, don't think that I'm saying this in-love sensation is wrong because it's not. I believe it is great and God given. But, after the wedding these important factors we overlook make it extremely difficult to have a successful marriage.

Most couples return from the honeymoon madly in love and eager for a successful relationship. It continues that way until they experience their first emotional conflict or clash of wills. Usually the first argument or lovers' quarrel isn't fatal, but most of the time it can leave a slight scar on the relationship.

I remember one of the first conflicts Charlotte and I experienced shortly after our marriage. I had joined the Air Force earlier that year and departed for training, leaving Charlotte to file our income taxes. Soon after we arrived at our first duty station in Panama City, Florida we received a letter from the Internal Revenue Service. Charlotte became fearful that she had done something wrong and we were in trouble. After reviewing the letter and realizing it was nothing, I decided to tease her and not let her read the letter which made her extremely upset. Now, I can't tell you why I did such a mean thing, but I thought it was fun at the time. Well, as you can imagine tempers ran high, her anger grew hotter and finally she threw a bowl filled with sugar at me. The worst part was we didn't have a vacuum cleaner to get the sugar out of the carpet and it attracted ants, which created another problem. I finally apologized for acting like a jerk and discovered that making up was so much fun!

Like most young couples do, we continued on our marital journey until we had another emotional eruption, followed by an exciting make-up session. Gradually these conflicts came closer and closer together as our wants, wills and desires clashed. If we had not been committed to God and each other these conflicts and differences could have done to our marriage what it is doing to so many today, turn a loving home into a "hell-on-earth." The question I have is why? Why can't couples recognize the likelihood for destruction that exists and detour around it? I found there are many answers to these questions depending on personalities, expectancy, attitude, and commitment of each person.

The problem with most newlyweds is they start out with a different road map for marriage. Each enters into marriage with a different set of directions. These differences are things like assumptions about roles, expectations about how to spend time and money, beliefs about children, not to mention the inherited baggage that follows us. But the one element that is most overlooked in marriages is the understanding of God's instructions for marriage and how to apply them in everyday life.

It's important that we recognize the one factor that can help assure a successful marriage and that is we should be believers of Jesus Christ. I've had people to tell me that you don't have to be a Christian to have a successful marriage. I have met many people who appeared to have a great relationship but once you get a close look you can see the unbalanced parts that will eventually eat away trust and love.

*   *   *

> ***One of the greatest factors in achieving the ultimate marriage relationship is being a follower of Jesus Christ.***

*   *   *

I can only speak from personal experience along with what I've read and heard from many marriage experts. I am fifty years old and I've been happily married for thirty of those years. I have three sons, two daughters-in-law, and two grandchildren. I have worked and/or lived in fifteen countries, counseled many couples, questioned

4

and documented hundreds of marriage situations, and I've never found one couple with a balanced, healthy, happy, fulfilled marriage that was not centered on Jesus Christ.

Therefore, knowing the principles that God gave us and seeing them work in thousands of situations to form a successful, lifelong marriage relationship, I believe I can accurately say one of the greatest factors in achieving the ultimate marriage relationship is being a follower of Jesus Christ. That is if you want your marriage to be victorious in every situation and raise a well-balanced, successful family.

Some people may misunderstand what being victorious, well-balanced and successful means. It doesn't mean you never have problems, arguments, disappointments and failures. It means you live by the principles that God put in place and you take the responsibility of your role as husband or wife and let God work in your marriage. Only then will you see the results that make marriage so wonderful and fulfilling.

As Christians, we should follow the instructions of Second Timothy chapter 2 verse 15 and strive to *"be diligent to present yourself approved to God..."* In the book of Hosea chapter 4 verse 6 it says, *"My people are destroyed for lack of knowledge."* With so many problems in marriages and many ending in divorce, we see more and more problems becoming evident.

We're experiencing problems such as loneliness, abuse, poverty, children with no home, or children trying to cope with broken families, not to mention the families living outside God's Will. The Bible will provide the knowledge to help us better understand our role as a spouse, parent and most of all as a Christian. God's Word will provide the direction for us to travel, the solutions for our current problems, and the power to overcome them in the future.

The family is designed by God Himself, but there's more to it than just the basic relationship. Many Christians know the Lord, but they are not living according to God's moral law, marital law, or family law. If we call ourselves Christians then why aren't we? Simply, we are not familiar with His Word or how to apply His Word to our lives. One other factor is very important even though it's controversial today, and that is being led by the Holy Spirit. It is one thing to possess the Spirit of God, to be a born-again believer, but a necessary second dimension can and should be discovered.

All Christians are familiar with the Holy Spirit but not all are controlled by, led by, or taught by the Holy Spirit. Consequently, a greater power to overcome the many attacks of the enemy on our relationships is absent, leaving us ill-equipped to succeed. You see, salvation will get you to heaven but allowing the Spirit to teach and lead you is the answer to being an over-comer, or as the Bible says in Romans chapter 8 verse 34, *"more than a conqueror."*

When we refuse to allow the Spirit total control in our lives we really are being disobedient to the plan of God. Disobedient believers will have discord in their families just as they will have discord in their own hearts, because there is discord between them and God. Being a Christian is definitely the starting point, but being filled with, counseled by, and taught by the Spirit makes the ideal a reality.

The first place I would like us to explore is Ephesians chapter 5, starting with verse 18 and continuing through chapter 6 verse 4. Paul puts being drunk on wine in opposition to being filled with the Spirit. Why? He wanted to help us understand what being filled really means. When you are drunk on wine, you are controlled by alcohol. Specifically, alcohol affects the control centers of the brain. As a result, intoxicated people may lose their self-control and behave different that others.

The same is true in a positive sense. When you are filled with the Spirit, you are allowing the Spirit to control you. We find that all the teaching on family in these scriptures flows from the power of the Spirit in verse 18 *"...but be filled with the Spirit."* The filling of the Holy Spirit produces at least three results: The first result we see is in verse 19, *"Speaking to yourselves in psalms and hymns and spiritual songs, singing and making melody in your heart to the Lord;"* this is how we should respond to being filled with the Spirit. The first thing we should possess is a sense of inner peace, inner contentment and joy that results in singing and feeling happy.

The next result we see is in verse 20 which says, *"Giving thanks always for all things to God the Father in the name of our Lord Jesus Christ;"* this is our response toward God. A Spirit-filled person not only sings within, but gives thanks to God every day for everything that comes their way.

And in verse 21 we see a Spirit-filled life directed toward others, *"Submitting to one another in the fear of God."* When a person has reverence accompanied with fear and stands in awe of God, that person really enters into worshiping Him. That person will be one who submits to others.

Submission is vital in the marriage and family as well as the church, and workplace. Most conflicts we experience come because we refuse to submit; we want to get the upper hand, we want our rights, we want our way, we want our opinion to dominate. But the Spirit-filled life is not a fight for the top; it's a fight for the bottom! It is the husband and wife not looking out for his or her own interest, but for the interest of the other.

Charlotte and I have devoted our lives to each other. We committed early on to make our marriage and family work at all cost. And I'll tell you the truth, it hasn't always been easy. But with the leading and teaching of the Holy Spirit we've come to understand that putting the other first is exactly what Jesus did when He chose the cross. He could have called thousands of angels to come to His rescue but instead He chose to submit to the Father's will. He gave His life so we could live not only eternally, but that we could have a life together as husband and wife filled with an abundance of love, joy, strength, and contentment.

*   *   *

A husband's submission to his wife does not mean that he relinquishes his responsibility of leadership in the home, but that he helps her to bear her burdens.

*   *   *

In today's "me generation" we've ignored, resisted, and tried to destroy the act of submission. But throughout scripture we are called upon to submit to one another. A couple of additional scriptures to study on submission are:

First Corinthians chapter 16 verse 16, *"...submit to such as these and to everyone who joins in the work, and labors at it."*

Hebrews chapter 13 verse 17, *"Obey your leaders and submit to their authority. They keep watch over you as men who must give an account. Obey them so that their work will be a joy, not a burden, for that would be of no advantage to you."*

But what does submission mean? It means to line up, to get in order, be arranged, to get in order under something or someone. A husband's submission to his wife does not mean that he relinquishes his responsibility of leadership in the home, but that he helps her to bear her burdens. He "gets underneath" to carry her cares; he's always ready to meet her needs and to sacrifice his own desires for what helps fulfill those needs.

It means sometimes, guys, we must give up a weekend golf game, ball game, or hunting trip to go with our wives to a social function, movie or reunion. Or maybe we just need to lay the remote down, turn the TV off, and listen. And ladies, it means that you must sometimes give up a shopping day, a new dress, or a favorite meal to go with your husband to purchase something he wants, or cook his favorite dish.

It's funny that during the courting days men say things such as, "Sure I'd love to go to the mall and watch you try on 15 or 20 dresses, I just love being with you, dear." And ladies, you are guilty also of saying things like, "Honey, I'd be glad to go with you to the ball game: it doesn't matter that its 30 degrees outside, I just want to be near you." We tend to put our best foot forward in the beginning, and then after marriage our true character becomes evident. And we tend to forget about submitting to each other.

*   *   *

Being submissive does not mean we're inferior to one another.

*   *   *

The Bible tells us that children are to submit also in obedience to their parents. And parents are to submit too. Ephesians chapter 6 verse 4 says *"And you fathers,* (can be translated also as parents*) do not provoke your children to wrath, but bring them up in the training and admonition of the Lord."* That means we are to get under our children and be caring, loving and supportive teachers. Wives are to submit to the loving leadership of their husbands. Husbands are called to bow to the needs of their wives. A father and mother are to bend to the sensitivity and needs of their children so that they don't provoke them to anger.

Every family member is an illustration of submission. There are homes where the husband understands the wife's submission but has no idea what it means for him to submit to her needs, to sacrifice himself for her. In those cases he has missed the point of Ephesians chapter 5 which calls us all at some point to submit to everyone else in the circle of our relationships. Being submissive does not mean we're inferior to one another. It means we're taking on the character of Christ – unconditional love.

And here we find another factor – love. No emotion is more needed, more talked about, and less understood than love. Poems by the hundreds have been written about it; stories, plays and movies have tried to demonstrate it; none of us ever tire of hearing about it. True love for your spouse is supernatural, a result of being filled with the fruit of the Spirit. That kind of love is a treasure that continues to grow and mature year after year. It doesn't depend on any single event but it takes a lifetime to be expressed. As the result of a man and woman sharing their total selves unconditionally, it can absorb conflict, disagreement, disappointment, tragedy, and even selfishness. It's not dependent on two perfect people, but on two people filled with the Spirit of God.

I can honestly say that after thirty years of marriage I love my wife Charlotte more than ever. She is my best friend and the one I'd rather spend time with than anyone else in the whole world. This doesn't mean we haven't had problems or disagreements and arguments. But our love is based on the love of God. Love is the ideal way to face the unknown and potentially bumpy road to the future. As Zig Ziglar says in his series "Courtship after Marriage," "Love is to marriage what shock absorbers are to a car – it cushions the rough spots in life (1)." This kind of love is evident when after years of marriage you still get butterflies in your stomach to see your mate drive up or the phone rings and you hear their voice and excitement begins to build in your body.

Falling in love is a wonderful experience, and where it is accompanied by modesty and restraint, God shares the joy of it. But God does not build a marriage upon the foundation of a mere natural attraction we call love. Dietrick Bonhoeffer, sitting in a Nazi prison cell, once wrote a wedding sermon for a niece who was about to be married. In it he said:

"Marriage is more than your love for each other. It has a higher dignity and power, for it is God's holy ordinance, through which he wills to perpetuate the human race till the end of time. In your love you see

12

only your two selves in the world, but in marriage you are a link in the chain of the generations, which God causes to come and to pass away to his glory, and calls into his kingdom. In your love you see only the heaven of your happiness, but in marriage you are placed at a post of responsibility toward the world and mankind. Your love is your own private possession, but marriage is more than something personal—it is a status, an office just as it is the crown, and not merely the will to rule, that makes the king, so it is marriage, and not merely your love for each other, that joins you together in the sight of God and man. As high as God is above man, so high are the sanctity, the rights, and the promise of love. It is not your love that sustains marriage, but from now on, the marriage that sustains your love."(2)

Now I don't want you to misunderstand me, love is an essential ingredient of marriage. But the marriage does not depend upon love for its continued existence. Rather, love should depend upon marriage for its continued existence. Mignon McLaughlin once wrote "A successful marriage is one in which you fall in love many times, always with the same person (3)." Couples who come to the conclusion that, "We just don't love each other any more," should be told "Start learning!" The reality is that in marriage we are not hostages of love. But we train love to be the willing servant in our marriage because love is a choice.

The Song of Solomon contains a beautiful picture of a right marriage relationship. Here you see a beautiful, tender love, with authority and submission quietly at work.

13

The great king is married to the Shulamite woman, and they are deeply in love. Notice how she describes her husband in Solomon chapter 2 verses 3-16.

> *"Like an apple tree among the trees of the forest is my lover among the young men. I delight to sit in his shade, and his fruit is sweet to my taste. He has taken me to the banquet hall, and his banner over me is love. Strengthen me with raisins, refresh me with apples, for I am faint with love. His left arm is under my head, and his right arm embraces me. Daughters of Jerusalem, I charge you by the gazelles and by the does of the field: Do not arouse or awaken love until it so desires. Listen! My lover! Look! Here he comes, leaping across the mountains, bounding over the hills. My lover is like a gazelle or a young stag. Look! There he stands behind our wall, gazing through the windows, peering through the lattice. My lover spoke and said to me, "Arise, my darling, my beautiful one, and come with me." See! The winter is past; the rains are over and gone. Flowers appear on the earth; the season of singing has come, the cooing of doves is heard in our land. The fig tree forms its early fruit; the blossoming vines spread their fragrance. Arise, come, my darling; my beautiful one, come with me."* (NIV)

She pictures him as her protector in verse 3. This woman finds shelter, protection, security, confidence, comfort, and contentment in her husband. She recognizes his leadership, but it all flows from their love, and there is nothing threatening for her in this relationship.

When a wife holds her husband in high esteem as in the Song of Solomon, and a man cherishes the wife God has honored him with, a reverence for the dignity and honor establishes their love on a foundation that will last forever. And it's on this foundation that we can find the kind of love which Paul describes in First Corinthians chapter 13, *"Love is patient, love is kind. It does not envy, it does not boast, it is not proud. It is not rude, it is not self-seeking, it is not easily angered, it keeps no record of wrongs. Love does not delight in evil but rejoices with the truth. It always protects, always trusts, always hopes, always perseveres..."(KJV)*

Let me ask a very important question. Husbands, what opportunities do you have every day to express the love of Christ toward your wife as the scripture describes in Ephesians chapter 5 verse 25, *"One who gave up His very life for His Bride?"* And wives, what opportunities do you have every day that you can give or express faithfulness to your husband that parallels what Paul described as the faithfulness of the Church to Christ in Ephesians chapter 5 verses 24 and 27, *"...subject in everything to Christ... without spot or wrinkle..., holy and without blemish!"* This is not merely an ideal to dream about, but it is the goal of the Holy Spirit with every Christian couple.

I've been a Christian and married over 30 years and I'm learning more and more every day what the Bible has to say about a meaningful marriage relationship. It's not easy today for husbands and wives to submit to one another in love and stay under the authority structure that God has designed for them. It isn't easy because to apply these principles is to go against human nature. We can be successful only to the degree that we are transformed by the Lord Jesus Christ and filled with the Holy Spirit.

What does God say about the marriage union? Is it just a contract or is it more? In our society today marriage does involve a civil contract, but this is only part of the entirety of marriage. According to God's Word, the marital relationship is really based on Covenant. But what is a covenant and what does it signify? In ancient times covenants were of three basic kinds.

1. **Covenant Between Equals.** In Genesis chapter 31 we find an example in the case of Laban and Jacob. Jacob having been victimized time and time again by his father-in-law Laban, decided to slip away with his family and flocks to avoid a confrontation. But when Laban caught up with him sparks flew. Finally, Laban offered a covenant of peace between the two of them. A pillar was set up to serve as a witness to the agreement that they would never again infringe upon each other's territory or property to do harm. They made vows, and called upon God to judge the one who broke covenant.

2. **Covenant Between a Weaker to a Stronger.** In Joshua chapter 9 verses 3-15 we see the Gibeonites plotting to deceive Israel and its leader Joshua because they were afraid and felt powerless before the awesome power of the Israelite army. They dressed as weary travelers from a distant

country, come to make a covenant or treaty with Israel. Once the covenant was made and the Israelite leaders discovered the deception, it was too late. They were obligated before God to honor its terms and not to destroy Gibeon. This was not a treaty between equals, but a petition by the weaker party to place its people under the protection of the stronger, Joshua and Israel's elders.

3. **Covenant Between a Stronger to a Weaker.** We find many times that a very powerful ruler would conquer lesser rulers and offer them peace and protection, in exchange for allegiance, financial and military support. These covenants were serious matters and included a detailed description of the obligations and stipulations as well as consequences if not adhered to.

Covenants through the Bible were extremely serious matters, so serious that God held guilty all those who violated the terms of a covenant. For instance, the Mosaic Covenant, given by God to the people of Israel, carried with it tremendous blessings for obedience and a curse on those who ignored its requirements. In Deuteronomy chapters 26-28 we can see a long list of blessings and curses of the covenant. What happened to those who failed to fulfill their part in God's covenants? I believe that Jeremiah, Hosea and Psalms clearly show us that we should not play games with God and His covenants.

"Both the house of Israel and house of Judah have broken the covenant I made with their forefathers. Therefore this is what the Lord says: I will bring on them a disaster they cannot escape." Jeremiah 11:10-11

"...the people have broken my covenant and rebelled against my law...now he will remember their wickedness and punish their sins." Hosea 8:1b, 13b

"But from everlasting to everlasting the Lord's love is with those who fear him, and his righteousness with their children's children – with those who keep his covenant and remember to obey his precepts." Psalm 103:17-18

From these and other passages, we are reminded that our Lord is always faithful to His covenants and expects us to be also. But how does marriage fit into the realm of covenant? Simply, it is the first covenant offered by God, the more powerful, to His human creatures, the weaker. Seeing that man was alone and incomplete, He formed a mate, not inferior to him or superior to him but different. With this helpmate God offered a permanent covenant of partnership with each other and with Him. He offered protection and blessing, children and grand-children; in short He offered them the basic building block of society – the home.

In exchange, God expects a permanent and faithful relationship to each other and to Him. He expects us to form a new mini-society, in which our children will leave father and mother and will cleave to each other, forming new and faithful building blocks for the generations that follow.

As with all covenants in the Bible, marriage fulfilled the same formula with a beginning, stipulations, blessings, curses, and witnesses. God is the originator of marriage and He witnesses the covenant as seen in Genesis chapters 1-3. Stipulations to the covenant include obeying His instructions, forming a new unit of society, being faithful to your spouse, and bearing children. Although curses are not specified in these passages of scripture, they are implied. Violation of any of God's ordinances brings His punishment on the offender.

But, does the Bible really call marriage a covenant? Yes, clearly He tells us that when a woman marries she enters a sacred covenant with God as well as with her husband. Proverbs chapter 2 verses 16-17 states, *"To deliver you from the immoral woman, from the seductress who flatters with her words, who forsakes the companion of her youth, and forgets the covenant of her God."* What does the Word say about the husband? Oh yes, in Malachi chapter 2 verse 14, *"...Yet you say, "For what reason?" Because the Lord has been witness between you and the wife of your youth, with who you have dealt treacherously; Yet she is your companion and your wife by covenant."*

When you study the scriptures you'll discover great insight into God's intentions for marriage and the home. But my point is that both husband and wife, obviously, are partners in a holy covenant, instituted by God and made in His presence. Let me also say that even though God hates divorce He doesn't hate the divorced person. We're all human and we're going to make mistakes. When we do, we are to ask forgiveness, repent, and move on for God.

My prayer is that God will bless you and your marriage relationship and that you will recognize and discover how to apply His principles to your life, marriage and vocation.

By answering the following questions and sharing them with your spouse you can better identify important issues and determine the steps necessary to improve your marriage relationship.

1. What background differences do we have?

_____

_____

_____

2. How might these background differences affect our marriage?

_____

_____

_____

3. What can I do to help prevent these differences from causing a problem?

_____

_____

_____

4. In what ways am I submissive to my spouse and family?

_____

_____

_____

5. What am I prepared to change to become submissive to God's principles of marriage?

_____

_____

_____

2

What on earth is expected of a Wife?

A young couple got married and went on their honeymoon. When they got back, the bride immediately called her mother. Well, said her mother, "how was the honeymoon?" "Oh, mama," she replied, "the honeymoon was wonderful! So romantic…" Suddenly she burst out crying. "But, mama, as soon as we returned, Sam started using the most horrible language – things I'd never heard before! I mean, all these awful 4-letter words! You've got to take me home…, PLEASE MAMA!" "Sarah, Sarah," her mother said, "calm down! You need to stay with your husband and work this out. Now, tell me, what could be so awful? What 4-letter words?" "Please don't make me tell you, mama," wept the daughter, "I'm so embarrassed, they're just too awful! Come get me, please!!" "Darling, baby, you must tell me what has you so upset. Tell your

23

mother these horrible 4-letter words!" Still sobbing, the bride said, "Oh, Mama…, he used words like: dust, wash, iron, cook!!!..." "I'll pick you up in twenty minutes" said mama.

I know many people may not think this is funny but the point is "expectations." What is expected of a wife? Too many marriages begin with wrong expectations which can cause heartache and difficulties in the relationship.   As the old saying goes, a woman marries a man thinking she can change him; and a man marries a woman hoping she'll never change. These problems can be avoided with clear communication about what each expects of the other in marriage.

*   *   *

> ***We don't expect to be instantly proficient in our vocation or careers so why should marriage be any different.***

*   *   *

Sometimes it takes a good counselor to help bring these areas to a couple's attention. I highly recommend that every couple get good Christian counseling before the wedding day arrives. If not, they'll end up needing it soon after the honeymoon, and then it's difficult for some to admit they need counseling. The word counseling to most means I don't know what I'm doing. I prefer to use the word education. If we're having problems lets learn more about marriage and what principles we should be living by to do it right.

If you think about it most couples say they are drawn together by the "in-love" sensation and they marry thinking everything from that point on will work great forever. Without study, experience, and guidance every couple will most likely have difficulty. We don't expect to be instantly proficient in our vocation or careers so why should marriage be any different. We study for years in school to learn a certain discipline. We have continuing education requirements for many vocations today, but we think marriage is supposed to be successful without it. I don't think so. If we want a marriage filled with love, respect, and trust we must study, learn, and practice.

The wife is not a slave, contrary to some chauvinistic, self-centered, egotistical husbands around the world. She is not standing around waiting for commands: "Do this; get that; go there; fix this!" The marriage relationship is much more intimate, personal and vital than that. Ephesians chapter 5 verse 22 indicates it by the words *"your own husband."* This phrase states devotion and a possessiveness, which assumes that a wife would willingly respond in submission to her "own" husband – one whom she possesses.

A couple we were friends with for a long time struggled with submission and expectations to the point of divorce. They seemed to have a happy marriage outwardly but once Charlotte and I began to spend time with them it was easy to see that a problem was mounting. They were a Christian couple; he was a teacher and leader in their church. He was a great provider, loving husband and father. She was a sweet, outgoing, likeable and intelligent woman. However, her expectations of him and failure to submit caused her to take advantage of his even-tempered, laid-back personality and put demands on him to take responsibility for every aspect of their life. Don't get me wrong, I believe the husband should take responsibility for his family, but he was not only providing for their every need, he was doing the cleaning of the house, the cooking, the lawn, maintaining the cars; she was living the life of me, me, me. She harped and nagged on him constantly.

*   *   *

In a family the wife should be the link between her husband and the children.

*   *   *

Once after visiting with them I told Charlotte if she treated me the way his wife treats him I would probably leave. He soon quit teaching the youth and eventually stopped attending church altogether. He finally became so frustrated with his home life he began to stop off at the local bar on his way home. As you can imagine, his getting home time became later and later. Life at home didn't get easier because she became enraged that he wasn't performing his duties like she expected. Eventually he began to see another woman. That other woman was his wife's friend. One who knew what he wanted and what his wife wasn't providing. To make a long story short, they divorced and went their separate ways and now both are re-married. Since their divorce both have stated they understand now where they went wrong.

I find that the Bible talks about "ladies" first when it speaks about God's order for the family. In a family the wife should be the link between her husband and the children. When she lives according to God's divine order, it will draw the husband and the children into order. Therefore, in speaking about divine order in the family, scripture addresses the wife first.

Most all Christian husbands are familiar with Ephesians chapter 5 verse 22, *"Wives submit to your own husbands as to the Lord."* But we fail most of the time to see just what submission really means, not just for the wife but for the husband also. In verse 21 Paul established the foundational principle of mutual submission that should characterize marriage and family life, *"Submitting to one another in the fear of God."* Here is the entrance that opens to specific commands addressed to the entire family; wives, husbands, children and parents.

To God, being submissive means to yield humble and intelligent obedience to an ordained power or authority. The example He gives is a Church being submissive to the rule of Christ, which is definitely not degrading. God didn't give this law of wives being submissive to their husbands because He didn't like women. He did this for the protection of women and the harmony of the home. God's

Word doesn't talk about a 50-50 democratic marriage. His order for the marriage relationship is for the wife to be 100% a wife and the husband is to be 100% a husband, but many couples have lost sight of or never understood what this means.

God has given wives the opportunity to choose freely the submissive role, even as Jesus chose to be submissive to the Father as stated in Philippians chapter 2 verses 5-9. *"Let this mind be in you which was also in Christ Jesus, who, being in the form of God, did not consider it robbery to be equal with God, but made Himself of no reputation, taking the form of a servant, and coming in the likeness of men. And being found in appearance as a man, He humbled himself and became obedient to the point of death, even the death of the cross. Therefore God also has highly exalted Him..."* God doesn't honor those who cling to their "rights," but those who choose freely to obey Him.

In Genesis chapter 3 the end of verse 16 God said, *"Yet your desire shall be for your husband, and he shall rule over you."* In Genesis chapter 2 verse 24 God also said that the husband and wife would be *"one flesh."* Yet, because of her unique creation, a wife is to be submissive to the headship of her husband. She is the one who is to be provided for, cared for, and secured by her husband.

I like how one minister explained the husband and wife relationship. He pointed out that "God made Eve from the rib of Adam not his foot or his head but his rib. The rib is what protects the heart; it's the part closest to the heart. Eve came from the side of Adam not underneath

28

or above him but from his side. That's why God called her a helpmate. The wife is a supportive, understanding, partner with equal recognition from God."

Life for me would be extremely difficult without Charlotte as my helpmate to give me support, assist in making decisions, help provide for our lifestyle and be a strong leader, teacher, and example for our sons and their wives. I know the issue of authority and submission is not popular today. Our generation has trouble accepting God's principles because we are a society deceived by a non-biblical philosophy of living and thinking. We have fallen prey to pushing for equal status and trying to erase all distinctions of the ministry of the Body of Christ. We need to examine God's word more clearly to clarify the matter of submission.

First Peter chapter 3 verse 1 says, *"Likewise, you wives, be submissive to your own husbands..."* Here again, the word submissive means "to come under in rank." It's a function word, not an essence word. It refers to how leadership should function in the home. Peter also emphasizes the possessiveness that softens the submissive role in *"your own husbands."* Therefore, because the husband is the wife's possession, submission should be a very welcomed response. Peter continues in verse 1 of chapter 3 by saying, *"that even if some do not obey the word, they, without a word, may be won by the conduct of their wives."* Here is a very important point that many wives overlook today. If your husband isn't living for God you must submit anyway. Instead of rebelling against his wishes, preaching at him and leaving him notes and gospel tracts, just love him and conform to God's pattern for marriage, and without even using the Word of God, you will win him to the Lord by your behavior.

One of the greatest examples of this principle is my mother and father. My mother gave her life to Christ many years before my father did. He drank alcohol almost every day and refused to attend church with her. Many Sundays he took her on the road, which hindered her from attending. For years she lived in a relationship that most would consider unnecessary and abusive.

I can remember one evening when I was eighteen years old asking mom to divorce dad and leave. I told her no one should have to put up with his way of life. But I thank God she understood what commitment meant and continued to pray for him and be that submissive, loving wife the Bible describes. Eventually her prayers and commitment paid off and my dad gave his heart to God. He told me later that he knew for years what he needed to do but wouldn't because he didn't think he was worthy. He said many times when things would get rough and times would take a turn for the worst, he would ask mom to pray and everything would turn around. Dad is with the Lord today, but the lessons God taught me through him and mom will be with me forever.

Many women have asked, exactly what kind of behavior are you talking about? According to verse 2 of First Peter chapter 3 it must be *"chaste conduct accompanied by fear (another translation says chaste and respectful)."* A wife should have respect for her husband. Not only is the wife to have pure behavior, conduct and living, she is to have a reverence, a sense of awe for her husband. When a wife is concerned with her husband, she respects him and her attitude will reflect her actions or activity.

*   *   *

Whatever you store up in your heart is what you will see come to reality in your life. So be careful what you say because you will experience the reality of your words.

*   *   *

I've heard many wives verbally degrade their husbands and speak negatively about them, even in the presence of their children. When a wife does this she is planting seeds of discord, mistrust, hatred, and abuse that will grow and manifest in her husband and children. Without realizing it she is the one who will be most hurt by her own destructive words.

Mark chapter 4 tells us an important principle about sowing and reaping. In this chapter Mark explains that our words are the seeds we sow and our heart is the ground where we sow them. In Matthew chapter 15 verse 18 we see the harvest we will get. *"But those things which proceed out of the mouth come from the heart, and they defile a man."* Another place to read and understand this principle is Luke chapter 6 verse 45 which says, *"A good man out*

31

of the good treasure of his heart brings forth good; and an evil man out of the evil treasure of his heart brings forth evil. For out of the abundance of the heart his mouth speaks." Whatever you store up in your heart is what you will see come to reality in your life. So be careful what you say because you will experience the reality of your words.

First Peter chapter 3 verse 3 goes on to talk about the outward activity of a wife. *"Do not let your beauty be that outward adorning of arranging the hair, of wearing gold, or of putting on fine apparel."* Our society today is so pre-occupied with the outward appearance that it has almost become a curse. I'm not saying that a wife should ignore her appearance. On the contrary, all wives should seek to be pleasing to their husbands because it brings joy to the husband for his wife to look good. But instead of focusing so much on the external as many do today, verse 4 says a woman should be concerned with *"the hidden person of the heart,"* or *"the secret of the heart."* In other words, don't work so hard on the outside, but work on the inside because the outward appearance will reflect the beauty of the inner spirit.

I have recognized the more Charlotte works on her inner spirit the more beautiful she becomes to me. As she grows in matters of the heart it begins to show in every area of her life, especially her outward appearance. If a wife really wants to be pleasing to her husband she must develop her inner spirit to the things of God and her outward response will become most attractive to her husband.

You're probably thinking what inward virtues should characterize such a woman? The scriptures say she will possess *"the incorruptible ornament of a gentle and quite spirit."* The Greek word for gentle means "silent or still." That's certainly unknown in our society today isn't it? But, nevertheless it is God's standard. The scriptures encourage women to adorn themselves in godliness, with a gentle and quiet spirit. That doesn't mean wives are just to vegetate and never offer an opinion. It does mean they are to be humble and still. Verse 4 describes a quiet spirit as being *"very precious (priceless) in the sight of God."*

I believe *"in the sight of God"* means "up close and personal or face-to-face." As a wife stands "face-to-face" with God, He doesn't see her hair or jewelry, He's looking for a gentle and quiet spirit. In His sight a wife with a gentle and quiet spirit is "precious." That rich word "precious" is used in Mark chapter 13 verse 3 when the woman opened the alabaster box and took out the priceless ointment. A gentle and quiet spirit is very valuable or priceless to God.

In verse 5 we are given some historical perspective, *"for in this manner, in former times, the holy women who trusted in God also adorned themselves, being submissive to their own husbands."* Holiness has always been the standard required by God. Holy women are preoccupied with God. Therefore, they adorned themselves with a gentle and quiet spirit and are submissive to their own husbands.

Peter focuses on Sarah the wife of Abraham in verse 6 because *"Sarah obeyed Abraham, calling him lord, whose daughters you are if you do good and are not afraid with any terror."* Another translation says, *"frightened by any fear."* If Abraham, according to Galatians chapter 3 verse 7, is the father of the faithful, then Sarah must be the mother of the submissive. Sarah had no fear in being submissive to Abraham. When holy women put their trust in God they have no fear of obeying God. If they're experiencing abuse they can be sure that God will take care of the results. Wives, as you obey God and submit to your husbands with a gentle and quiet spirit, you can know that God will honor your obedience—no matter what.

In Titus chapter 2 we find another key passage that teaches us about God's order for women and wives. Verse 3 says *"The older women likewise, that they be reverent in behavior, not slanderers, not given to much wine, teachers of good things."* Again we see that the older women are to have respect and speak well of their husbands. They are to teach the younger women "to love their husbands." Wives should be characterized by love for their husbands.

Verse 4 adds that young women should be taught *"to love their children."* Love is self-sacrifice. In John chapter 15 verse 13 Jesus said that the greatest act of love is giving yourself. Wives are to do everything possible to meet the needs of their husbands and children. Verse 5 of Titus chapter 2 goes on to say that young women must be taught *"to be discreet, chaste, homemakers, good, obedient to their own husbands, that the word of God may not be blasphemed."* Another translation puts it this way, *"sensible, pure, workers at home, kind, being subject to their own husbands, that the word of God may not be dishonored."* Here is the real issue. God wants His Word to be glorified, and when we do not live by that Word we dishonor it.

For the woman today who says she can't be submissive because she must be fulfilled, worthy and respected for her mind, ability, and activity, I want you to meet an industrious woman. And if you think a woman is stifled in her God-ordained role, take a close look at this amazing passage of scripture in Proverbs chapter 31 starting with verse 10 and continuing through verse 31. These verses will illustrate the true character of a Christian wife and mother.

Verse 10 – *"Her worth is far above rubies."* She is valuable to God, her husband, children and community.

Verse 11 – *"The heart of her husband safely trusts her, so he will have no lack of gain."* Her husband can trust her with the finances without any fear she will waste their money or squander their resources. She is trustworthy.

Verse 12 – *"She does him good and not evil all the days of her life."* She sees herself as one who supports her husband to help free him from anxiety and fear. She is very supportive.

Verse 13-14 – *"She is like the merchant ships, she brings her food from afar."* In fact, if she has to travel like a merchant's ship to bring it from afar she does (14). And according to verse 19, she puts it on the spindle and the distaff and makes thread. And with that thread she makes necessary things. In other words she is productive! All this comes short of saying that a woman must stay at home and never leave. She may have a career, a ministry, disciple people, attend school, shop, plus many other things that require her leaving her home. Obviously, there are things to do and places to go if she wishes to be productive.

Verse 15 – *"She also rises while it is yet night, and provides food for her household, and a portion for her maidservants."* She has more concern for her family than for her own comfort.

Verse 16-19 – *"She considers a field and buys it."* She buys a field, purchases the seed, and plants a vineyard. There is a place for enterprise, but her home is the base. The wife is not to be the total source of the family's income as wives are in many homes today, but she is prosperous.

Verse 17 – *"She girds herself with strength, and strengthens her arms."* Such women are not frail and self-indulgent but are working with their hands to provide the necessities of the home, not only because they need it for the moment, but also because she's planning for the future, against the moment when tragedy might come."

Verse 25 in Hebrew says, "She'll laugh at the future."

Verse 20-21 – *"She extends her hand to the poor"* A progression appears in these verses, which spell out another reason she does all this. She does it so that she can give to those who have nothing. She also provides scarlet clothing for her household to protect them from the cold weather (21). And when the needs of the poor and the needs of her family are met, she makes herself a lined overcoat out of tapestry (22). It is a garment of function and unusual beauty. Finally, in verse 24, after she has met the needs of her family, the poor and herself, she starts a little business selling fine linen and delivering belts to the merchant. And that, too, is found in the right sequence of priorities.

Verse 27-28 – The result is *"She watches over the ways of her household, and does not eat the bread of idleness. Her children rise up and call her blessed; her husband also, and he praises her."* There is the prize; all the result of God's perfect plan and design.

This wife is creative, helpful, insightful, loving and obedient to God and her husband. She is a wife, mother, supervisor, business woman, problem solver and very prosperous in everything she attempts. She is held in high regard by her friends, employees and family. Is there anything more a woman would want in life?

A wife's primary responsibility is to give of herself, her time, and her energy to her husband, children and home. This does not mean that women cannot have responsible positions of leadership and still be in God's plan. God seems to have peculiar honors for women. They were the last to linger at the cross and the first to come to the tomb. There are many examples such as Mary Magdalene who first appeared after His resurrection; Miriam, who was instrumental in saving Moses' life; Deborah, who gave leadership to the Israelites as prophetess and judge; and Esther, the courageous queen who saved her people from death.

The New Testament also speaks of prophetesses, such as the widow Anna, and the unmarried daughters of Philip, and a businesswoman named Lydia who was one of the early converts under Paul's ministry. But the one who is "blessed among women," the most honored woman of all time, the mother of our Lord was just a humble woman who found fulfillment as a wife and mother in the home where God had set her.

Let me give you an example of how God takes care of wives who try to make right decisions. Several years ago Charlotte worked in the business development department for a large financial services institution. Our son Brad was in the eighth grade and on the junior-high football team. The team was having an outstanding season, and four of his games were out of town requiring us to depart early in the afternoon to arrive on time to see him play.

Charlotte asked her supervisor for permission to leave work an hour early on those four days. She was told yes at first and the next day her boss changed his mind and said no. He explained that if he allowed her he would have to allow others to do the same and he couldn't do that. She came home frustrated and said, "I have to choose between my child and this bank and I choose my child." The next day she went in and informed her boss that she understood his position but this was her resignation and she would be leaving in two weeks. He was flabbergasted! She said his chin dropped on the desk as she left his office.

To show you how God honors right priorities, two weeks later she cleaned out her desk and departed that company. However, the following Monday she went to work for another company, closer to home, earning more money with less working hours. God is good and He will always reward those that put Him first and prioritize according to His divine order.

By answering the following questions you can better recognize actions and identify ways to improve your marriage relationship. If you'll share your answers with your spouse you both can begin to understand your needs, wants and desires.

1. What do I expect from my husband?

_____

_____

_____

2. What does my husband expect from me?

_____

_____

_____

3. In what ways do I show support for my husband and how can I improve?

_____

_____

_____

4. What examples did I have growing up?

       Father   Mother

_____

_____

_____

_____

5. What could I do to be more attractive to my husband?

_____

_____

_____

6. In what ways does my job/career require me to perform/behave that would be displeasing to God and my husband? If none, great. If so, how do I change?

_____

_____

_____

3

What is a Husband to do?

After 17 years of marriage, a man dumped his wife for a younger woman. The downtown luxury apartment was in his name and he wanted to live there with his new love so he asked the wife to move out and he would buy her another place to live. The wife agreed to this, but asked that she be given 3 days by herself, to pack up her things. While he was gone the first day she lovingly put her personal belongings into boxes, crates and suitcases.

On the second day, she had the movers come and collect her things. On the third day, she sat down for the last time at their candlelit dining room table, soft music playing in the background, and feasted on a pound of shrimp and a bottle of Chardonnay. When she had finished, she went into each room and deposited a few of the resulting shrimp shells into the hollow of the curtain rods. She then cleaned up the kitchen and left.

The husband came back, with his new girlfriend. All was bliss for the first few days, then it started, slowly but surely. Clueless, the man could not explain why the place smelled so bad. They tried everything, cleaned and mopped and aired the place out. Vents were checked for dead rodents, carpets were steam cleaned, air fresheners were hung everywhere. Exterminators were brought in, the carpets were replaced, and on it went.

Finally, they could take it no more and decided to move. The moving company arrived and did a very professional packing job, taking everything to their new home, including the curtain rods.

The great English war hero Field Marshal Montgomery once said to his young troops, "Gentleman, don't even think about marriage until you have mastered the art of warfare! (4)" A great number of men may think they can relate to that statement. But the question I have is why does marriage have such great potential for warfare? Why does it seem to be so hard to have a dynamic love relationship with another person?

One of the most promising relationships is that which occurs between a man and a woman in marriage, yet the realization of achieving it can be so elusive. It's becoming increasingly rare to have a significant, lasting relationship with someone, to have a marriage that gets better, richer, and more fulfilling. In fact marriage today is portrayed as a fighting, unfaithful, discontented, bitter relationship with half of them ending in separation or divorce.

The state of married relationships today can be traced back to Genesis chapter 2 verse 18 where God *said "it is not good that man should be alone; I will make him a helper comparable to him."* In verses 21-22 God provided this helper to aid Adam as he ruled creation. From the very beginning God designed someone to be in charge and someone to help; someone to be in authority and someone to submit to that authority; someone to be the provider, and someone for whom to provide. It was a wonderful, perfect relationship. Adam viewed Eve in every sense as one with him—that was God's design. He was the leader and she was to follow his lead, but in such perfect balance that the roles are really lost within their oneness. The woman's submissiveness and the man's provision were both willing and beautiful. There was no animosity, no struggle, and no conflict—only a glorious union.

But something monumental occurred in Genesis chapter 3. The serpent bypassed the headship of the man and went to the one who was by design the follower. He enticed Eve to do the one thing God had told them not to do – eat of the fruit of the tree of the knowledge of good and evil (Gen 2:17). She ate it and then convinced Adam to eat it. Here we see the reversal of their roles.

We continually ask the question, "How could this happen?" Well, from years of study we know more about the human body and human make-up than ever before. And we know that God made man and woman different with different needs, and some believe this is what satan used to deceive Eve. Let me explain. Men in general are more visually oriented than women. Because of that we can say that a man is turned-on more by sight than anything else, making him more of a see-do kind of person. Women on the other hand are more intellectual; they are moved more by words and physical touch. Therefore we can say a woman is more of a hear-feel kind of person. God made us with this need so we would feed off each other to fill this void.

*　　*　　*

To have a marriage that works today there are two things needed, a woman characterized by submission, and a man characterized by sacrificial love.

*　　*　　*

The man, Adam, was excited by the most beautiful thing on earth – the woman Eve. The woman Eve was ignited by the man, Adam, his presence and his sharing of information about what God had told him of the garden and the world.

Some believe this is where the enemy moved in because there is no evidence in scripture where Adam relayed all the information about the entire garden to Eve. Therefore, satan used this need for information to deceive her. Some think because Adam loved her so much he knew she would be taken from him, so he agreed to eat the fruit of the tree of knowledge of good and evil. By doing so he gave up dominion of this world to satan. The woman took over the leadership of the man, and man became the follower. Regardless of satan's avenue in deceiving Eve, God's design for marriage was twisted at that moment of temptation, and the defilement of the marriage relationship began.

Satan has been using this same technique ever since. When a husband doesn't fulfill his wife's needs it becomes easier for her to look elsewhere to have those needs met. The same goes for the wife. She must fill the void in her husband's life because the enemy will always find someone to meet those needs and bring division in the home.

To have a marriage that works today there are two things needed: 1) a woman characterized by submission, and we've already talked a little on this subject; and 2) a man characterized by sacrificial love, whose commitment is to love his wife and provide for her everything he would for himself – as was true before the fall. This can be accomplished only through clear understanding and divine power. Husbands find it very hard to love their wives because it isn't natural. It's natural for men to love themselves, to be self-consumed, self-preoccupied, and self-absorbed.

Ephesians chapter 5 verses 25-33 tells us exactly what we are to do: *"Husbands, love your wives, just as Christ also loved the church and gave Himself for it; that He might sanctify and cleanse it with the washing of water by the word, that He might present it to Himself a glorious church, not having spot or wrinkle or any such thing, but that it should be holy and without blemish. So husbands ought to love their own wives as their own bodies. He who loves his wife loves himself; for no one ever hated his own flesh, but nourishes and cherishes it, just as the Lord does the church. For we are members of His body, of His flesh and of His bones. For this reason a man shall leave his father and mother, and be joined to his wife; and the two shall become one flesh. This is a great mystery; but I speak concerning Christ and the church. Nevertheless let each one of you in particular so love his own wife as himself, and let the wife see that she respects her husband."*

If you ask the average husband, "Do you love your wife?" he'll reply "Of course I do!" In saying this, he means what he feels toward her or maybe what he does for her, in the way of care and consideration. But the love Paul speaks about in Ephesians chapter 5 verse 25 and Colossians chapter 3 verse 20 is measured not by what a husband feels nor by what he directly does. Rather, it is measured by the sacrifice of himself.

The New Testament being translated from Greek we find there are four different and distinct words in Greek that are all translated by the single English word, "love." We must understand them if we are to see exactly what Paul was telling us.

- The first word, *Storge`*, conveys the idea of fondness, devotion, or connectedness within a family as in Romans chapter 12 verse 10.

- The second is *Eros* which indicates physical intimacy or sexual love. Our word erotic comes from this word. But, there are no New Testament uses of this word.

- Next is *Phileo* which is Greek for companionship in a sense of human affection and concern; our word "philanthropy" comes from this word. Jesus used this word in John chapter 15 verses 13-15 when he called the disciples his friends, not his servants. Again this word is used in John chapter 11 verses 3 and 26 when referring to the love Jesus had for Lazarus.

- Last and most important is *Agape*. This is a love measured by sacrifice. It is the strongest, most intimate, most far-reaching, and most qualitative term for love. This is the word used in the New Testament to describe the love of God and the love he reproduces in men. This is the love of John chapter 3 verse 16, Romans chapter 5 verse 5, and First Corinthians chapter 13. It is this word which Paul uses when he says, *"Husbands, love your wives."* And he clearly means a love ready to sacrifice.

The most obvious expression of love is the husband's financial support of the family. A sign of the moral breakdown in our homes today is the husband relinquishing this responsibility to the wife. Working wives and working mothers have become so much a part of our culture that we don't stop to consider what a departure this is from divine order or the harmful effect it is having upon our family and home.

*   *   *

A husband who takes seriously his role in God's order for the family does not take for granted his wife's relationship with Jesus.

*   *   *

A husband who loves his wife according to scripture will give first priority to her spiritual needs. A husband's first concern should be that his wife is rightly related to the Lord. He needs to recognize that real happiness and fulfillment for her as a woman, wife, and mother must be built upon a solid foundation of a relationship with Jesus.

God has entrusted the wife to the husband as a holy thing. It is his responsibility to do everything possible for her to be preserved holy, established and perfected in holiness. No one can be a bigger hindrance to a woman in spiritual things than her husband. But also no one can encourage her more to advance in all that is good as he can.

A husband who takes seriously his role in God's order for the family does not take for granted his wife's relationship with Jesus. He recognizes his call under God to be a spiritual "head" to his wife. As Christ is responsible for the care and growth of the Church, the husband is responsible for the spiritual care and growth of his wife and family. This is unmistakable in scripture.

An international survey cited in "The Seven Stumbling Blocks Ahead of Husbands,"[5] published by The American Institute of Family Relations indicates the seven most common failings of husbands, in the opinions of wives:

1. A lack of tenderness
2. A lack of politeness
3. A lack of sociability
4. A failure to understand the wife's temperament and peculiarities
5. Unfairness in financial matters
6. Frequency of snide remarks and sneers at the wife before company or the children
7. A lack of plain honesty and truthfulness

Men must recognize that their wives are precious gifts from God as Proverbs chapter 18 verse 22 tells us. In Ephesians chapter 5 verses 25-33 God calls men to love their wives in a way that imitates Christ loving the church. The wife's greatest need is for intimacy, and I'm talking about oneness, not sex. She wants her husband to give her first place in his life as Genesis chapter 3 verse 16b explains - after God, but before all others. Men, make her your top priority. Here are a few suggestions on how to do that:

1. **<u>Be her best friend:</u>** You and she are the only ones in this together; everyone else comes and goes including your children. To become best

friends takes spending time with each other so guard your time jealously. Husbands seem to make time for everything and everyone else and we must do the same for our spouse if our relationship is a priority and it should be.

2. **Make deposits into her "emotional bank account."** Encourage her with words. Hold her hand, rub her shoulders, give her hugs, and tell her you love her. (Don't be like the man who hadn't told his wife he loved her since the wedding. When she asked him if he still loved her he said, "I told you 20 years ago I did, and if it changes I'll let you know.") She needs to be reassured of that love over and over again.

3. **Spend time with her alone.** Develop shared interests. Talk to her about what's in your heart, and find out what's in her heart. What is it that she wants in life? What's her greatest characteristic? What's her weakness, and how can you help her more in becoming the woman God wants her to become. Schedule events for the two of you to attend. Surprise her with little gifts. Take her on dates. No matter how long you've been married take her to restaurants with soft candlelight and set in the corner and flirt with her. The magic that got you together is still there. Enjoy it!

4. **Listen to her deeply.** No relationship can thrive without communication. Take time to hear and understand. Do more than look at her when

she is talking. Listen to what she is saying, and respond in a manner that confirms you really care. I'm not talking about during commercial breaks on television or while you're paying the bills. Take time to listen and remind her how much you depend on her.

5. **<u>Dream together about the future.</u>** When you first committed to each other you had dreams about what you wanted in the future. You wanted a certain kind of home, family, and career. Maybe you've achieved it all, and maybe not. But wherever you are now, don't stop dreaming about where you want to be together tomorrow.

6. **<u>Remember the little things.</u>** Send her romantic notes or emails. Send her flowers, not for any special occasion, just because. Compliment her on the things she does or how she looks. Hold her hand when you're out running errands. You'd be surprised how these little things can keep the romance alive in your marriage. It's truly amazing to meet the love of your life, but it's even more wonderful to make that love last a lifetime.

The last thing I would like to address is praying with and for your wife. A successful marriage is always a triangle: A husband, a wife, and God. When a husband and wife seek God they not only grow closer to God, but closer together, and the closer they grow to God, the less outside influences are able to have an effect on them.

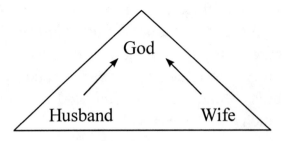

A key element in strengthening your marriage is prayer. Paul says in Colossians chapter 1 verse 9 that he *"does not cease to pray for you"* referring to the Christians at Colosse. By his example we see the importance of praying daily for the people you love. In this passage Paul shows us a number of concerns we should pray for.

1. **<u>Pray for your wife to know the Will of God for her life</u>** (verse 9). Paul prays first that the people he loves will be filled with the knowledge of God's will. Paul is saying, "I want you to know and experience the will of God." There is nothing more important than praying for your wife and family – their salvation, sanctification, and their growing in the things of God.

2. **<u>Pray for her lifestyle</u>** (verse 10). It is so easy today to become stagnant in our walk with Jesus Christ. Pray for your wife that she will have vibrancy and will not fall into a mere status quo relationship with God. Pray that her character will not only please the Lord, but that she will also bear fruit and good works in everything she attempts for His glory and honor. Pray that she

will grow and be productive and have a strong ministry to her family and others.

3. <u>**Pray for her to have the ability to overcome difficult situations**</u> (verse 11). We live in a morally and socially complex society which bombards our families with mixed signals and complicates our walk with God. So husbands need to pray for their wives and children not to be overcome with temptations, but that they will be strengthened for spiritual battles in crisis situations. Pray for God's protection to be on them each day. Pray for His angels to have charge over her and for His angels to go before her and prepare the way for her everyday. Today marriages are under attack like never before, and we must wage war against the spiritual forces of evil.

4. <u>**Pray that her attitude will be joyful and thankful**</u> (verses 11 & 12). Pray that she will rejoice in all the things God has given her to do, and that she will see the positive side of God's grace and be thankful for His mercy in your lives. Having a positive attitude is a major factor to being successful in the goals we set. As a husband you have the ability to be the greatest motivator to your wife. You are the key to her being positive and thankful.

5. <u>**Pray with your wife**</u>. Many couples find it easy to pray for each other but difficult to pray

together. Hearing your spouse pray for you has great power. It is not only uplifting but it opens the door for understanding, intimacy and trust. It also closes the door for the enemy to use to infiltrate your mind with lies about the love your spouse has for you.

Prayer is the one thing that we <u>must</u> do as husbands and in fact, it is required by God. We are the priests of the household and a priest not only ministers to the needs of his household, but he also carries those needs to God on behalf of his household.

According to Solomon in Ecclesiastes chapter 1 verses 9 says, *"That which has been is what will be, that which is done is what will be done, and there is nothing new under the sun."* Also Isaiah chapter 46 verses 9 and 10 say, *"remember the former things of old...declaring the end from the beginning..."* In other words if we want to know what to do today we must look to the past because everything in scripture is a type and shadow of things to come.

*   *   *

The divorce rate in the marriages where the husband and wife pray together on a consistent basis was one in eleven thousand.

*   *   *

Therefore, once again let us look at Abraham and Sarah. In Genesis chapter 12 we find that Abraham is called by God to take his wife, leave his homeland, and go to a land he does not know. In all his journeys I find something very interesting. Everywhere he went he built an altar of prayer to God with the exception of two places. When he went to Egypt in chapter 12, and when he went to Gerar in chapter 20, he failed to build an altar. At both places his wife, Sarah, was taken from him and ended up living with the king, separated from Abraham. I believe this is a great example for us today of what is necessary to keep our marriages together. We must put an altar of prayer in the home. And it is the husband's responsibility to do so and to carry all things to God, especially the welfare of his family.

The divorce rate today in America is somewhere around fifty percent and one source says the divorce rate in the church is even greater. Another source cited by one of my favorite teachers in his book, *Proving God,* said that the divorce rate in the marriages where the husband and wife prayed together on a consistent basis was one in eleven thousand (6). Now I'm no genius, but I believe this tells me what will keep a marriage together – <u>PRAYER</u>!

Prayer is one of the most important factors to living a successful life and for a husband it is vital. First Peter chapter 3 verse 7 says, *"Likewise you husbands, dwell with them with understanding, giving honor to the wife, as to the weaker vessel, and as being heirs together of the grace of life, that your prayers may not be hindered."* I certainly don't want my prayers to be hindered. I want God to hear and respond when I pray. Therefore, I must follow this principle, and give honor to my wife and treat her as the loving mate God blessed me with.

Let me expound on one thing before we move on. In many homes today the husband will not pray for his family. Not because he doesn't love them, but in most cases he has no relationship with God and therefore does not know the benefits or the consequences of not doing so. If this is the case then it's the wife's responsibility to keep an altar of prayer in the home. And above everything she should pray for the husband to accept his responsibility and build a relationship with Jesus Christ.

I have one more thing that I think is important to mention before closing this chapter. Jesus gave us all the principles necessary to live a life of health, wealth, and happiness today. But, He also gave us some examples that I think are noteworthy for fathers.

In Matthew chapter 24 verse 37 Jesus said, *"But as the days of Noah were, so also will the coming of the Son of Man be. For as in the days before the flood, they were eating and drinking, marrying and giving in marriage, until the day that Noah entered the ark."* And in Luke chapter 17 verse 28 He also said *"Likewise as it was also in the days of Lot..."*

I believe Jesus is telling us in these scriptures that Noah and Lot are two examples of fathers we see today. Both of these men were righteous in the sight of God. But both chose different paths. Noah listened to God. He had a passion to obey God no matter what others thought. He trusted God for his provision. He led his family to safety when everyone else was being destroyed by the flood.

Lot on the other hand looked more at material possessions for security and safety. When he separated from Abraham he chose to live near to the cities of Sodom and Gomorrah where the grass was green and there was plenty of water available. However, he ended up living in the city of Sodom and losing influence with his own family. His children didn't even believe him when he attempted to convince them to depart the city before it was to be destroyed by God.

These two examples should help fathers today to choose obedience to God and be the example for their families. If we do as Lot did and look only at the material things we stand to lose everything, including our children.

My prayer is that the Holy Spirit of God would invade every home and begin to open the eyes of every husband to see what God has given him, and do what is right in the sight of God. Every husband should dedicate his life to God, love his family, take responsibility to provide (food, shelter, love, respect and guidance) for his family, respect all others as being God's creation, and use the gifts and abilities God has placed in him to accomplish great things in his life. There is nothing greater than living for God, loving your wife and raising godly children to grow up and become like you.

Below are more questions to answer and discuss with your spouse to help you become more aware of your actions and improve your marriage and your future.

1. What do we argue about and why?

   _____

   _____

   _____

2. In what ways do I show commitment to my wife?

   _____

   _____

   _____

3. How do I support my wife spiritually and how can I improve?

   _____

   _____

   _____

4. In what ways can I express to my wife that she is top priority to me?

_____

_____

_____

5. How do I show my wife I love her and how can I improve?

_____

_____

_____

4

Don't blame the kids

I want to start by borrowing an often-used story about a frog that was put into a shallow pan of cool water, a pan from which the frog could have easily jumped out. Very slowly the water was heated. Almost undetectably the temperature began to rise, gradually reaching the boiling point. The frog continued to sit in the pan, seemingly unaware of the rising temperature, until he was boiled to death. At any point he could have jumped out and avoided his fate, but the increase in temperature was so gradual he didn't even notice!

That's what has happened in many cases to the family today. We have been sitting in what was at first a rather "cool" environment, a country that was founded on spiritual beliefs and favorable to spiritual things. While we have been content to sit comfortably in the system, the water has been gradually heating up. The family unit is being destroyed. The Christian families should have jumped out of the "pan" long ago. We knew we'd been in the pan too long when we discovered that the divorce rate among Christians was higher than it was for non-Christians.

The time has come to do something except sit while our families are being ripped apart by this world's system. God is calling us to be different from the world around us. We should have unique marriages, unique families, and unique life-styles which set us apart from the world. In Ephesians chapters 4 and 5 Paul said that we are not to walk as the heathen walk. We are to walk in love, not in lust; in light, not in darkness; in wisdom, not in foolishness; and in the Spirit, not in the flesh.

In Leviticus chapter 18 God laid down the law of behavior for Israel, which called for them to be separate from the world. In verse 26 He says, *"You shall therefore keep my statutes and my judgments, and shall not commit any of these abominations, either any of your own nation or any stranger who sojourns among you."* And verse 30 repeats, *"Therefore you shall keep my ordinance, so that you do not commit any of these abominable customs which were committed before you, and that you do not defile yourselves by them: I am the Lord your God."* God has maintained this desire for separation and distinction for His children through all His revelation.

God is still giving us the same message today in Ephesians chapter 6 as in Leviticus chapter 18: "Do it my way. Don't listen to what the world says. You're not of the world anymore, you have overcome it. This is my standard." Clearly, it has always been God's intention for His people to be distinct, set apart, not pliable to the pressure applied by the world, not conforming to the world system. And unless we meet His standard now in our own homes, we have nothing to pass on to the next generation so they can live to the glory of God.

There is an old Chinese proverb, which says, "One generation plants the trees and the next gets the shade." We are living in the shade of a "tree" planted in the past by men and women who had high moral standards, godly principles, and Christian values. What are we planting in our generation for the shade of the next generation? What are we planting to protect our children from this world's deceptive system? We cannot just sit idly by and think that our children and future generations will turn out fine on their own. Until we come out of the world and begin to be separated and teach a biblical pattern of living to our children, we will have nothing for the next generation.

Our world today doesn't seem to want to be bothered with children anymore. This is extremely hard to understand because the scriptures are very clear that God gives children – they are a gift from His hand. Many passages confirm this truth:

1. "God is the source of our children according to:

   Gen 4:1, 25 *"...I have gotten a man from the Lord."*

   Gen 4:25 *"...God has granted me another son... "(NLT)*

   Gen 16:10 *"...I will give you more descendants that you can count..."(NLT)*

Gen 17:16 *"...I will bless her and I will give you a son by her."*

Gen 29:31 *"When the Lord saw that Leah was not loved, he opened her womb..."*

Ruth 4:13 *"...and the Lord enabled her to conceive, and she gave birth to a son."*

1 Sam 1:19-20 *"...Elkanah lay with Hannah his wife, and the Lord remembered her. So in the course of time Hannah conceived and gave birth to a son."*

2. Children are a heritage or a reward from the Lord.

Palm 127:3, *"Sons are a heritage from the Lord, children a reward from him"*

3. Children are to be a source of joy.

Psalm 113:9, *"He settles the barren woman in her home as a happy mother of children."*

Psalm 127:4-5, *"Like arrows in the hands of a warrior are sons born in one's youth. Blessed is the man whose quiver is full of them. They will not be put to shame when they contend with their enemies in the gate."*

Pro 23:24, *"The father of a righteous man has great joy; he who has a wise son delights in him."*

God gives children as a blessing, a benediction, and a grace to life. Children bring great potential for happiness, but only if they are raised in righteousness as Proverbs chapter 23 and verse 24 tells us.

A 19-year-old sums up the legacy from his parents with this tragic letter to U.S. News and World Report (7):

I am a 19-year-old who kept a bottle under the front seat of the car the last two years of high school. While reading your special report, "Troubled Teenagers," a single thought came to mind: You can get every psychologist in the book to dig up examples and statistics and all you have are examples and statistics. I appreciate your effort, but just look at it this way:

Post-World War II parents started in the world of liberal giveaways while trying to keep up the harsh discipline that they grew up with a "free world" and a prison at home. The rebellious teenagers of the 50's and 60's went to "love-ins" and became the confused parents of the 70's, the decade when everyone went to their shrink.

Vietnam blew away the glory and majesty of the leader of the free world. The economy is shot, the family unit is in trouble, respect for authority is a joke. For the right price, you can buy yourself a senator or a judge, or he is out buying himself a 16-year-old to use for a couple of hours. Money is worthless, but you're worthless without it.

If the social scientists won't figure us out, maybe they should try to grow up in the world we've been stuck in… knowing why things happen might satisfy your curiosity, but it doesn't do us any good. Stop worrying about why your son needs a drink before he can face his morning classes, or why your daughter went out and got pregnant. Just help them cope with the reality of it.

Before throwing us into categories, just remember that we have got to run this joint in 30 years when you die off or retire and starve on Social Security. I leave it up to you: Either give us a little help and understanding, or put the world out of its misery and send up the missiles, and hope mother nature has better luck with the next thing that crawls up out of the slime.

Even though this letter was written a number of years ago this teen, like so many teenagers today, was truly hurting and would have gladly received a dad and mom that would listen and understand. How many of our children are in similar situations today? It may not be drinking, or sex, or drugs, but they are dealing with an evil system that satan is using to destroy everyone that he can lure his way.

So what are parents to do? First we must recognize that there are causes of the present chaos in our homes and we must commit to take action to change what is happening. I want to share some of the reasons that have been provided by two different sources: a law enforcement agency and a Christian psychiatrist.

The Houston, Texas Police Department published a leaflet called "How to Ruin Your Children,"[8] which was guaranteed to be 99% effective. In part it said:

1. Begin with infancy to give your child everything he/she wants.
2. When they pick up bad words, laugh at them.
3. Never give them any spiritual training. Let them wait until their 20's and decide for themselves.
4. Avoid using the word "wrong." It may develop a serious guilt complex.
5. Pick up everything they leave lying around so they will be experienced in throwing responsibility on everybody else.

This may sound comical to some but the facts speak for themselves. If we use this behavior in raising our children we're opening the door for an evil system to destroy their future, steal their joy in life and kill any hope they could have had for success.

The one thing that many parents have misunderstood and disagreed upon is discipline. When we *"spare the rod, we spoil the child."* (Proverbs 13:24) I know there are many who differ when it comes to raising children especially in this area, but we are not showing our children love if we do not provide guidelines and limits for them to live within. There is no set standard for discipline because every child is different with different personalities and characteristics. Therefore, each requires disciplining in a different manner.

I know with my three sons each required a different measure of discipline. Brad, the oldest, needed the rod applied often to help him understand that there are limits and you must stay within them. Josh, our second son, required less than Brad. Simply asking Josh was enough most of the time. He understood the consequences and behaved accordingly. Our third son Tyler required much less discipline than Josh. Talking with him and explaining the guidelines and limitations was enough.

Dr. Paul D. Meier, in his book *"Christian Child-Rearing and Personality Development,"*(9) explores the tragedy of children raised without concern for divine standards. He does it by showing, in a startling way, how to raise certain kinds of children. For example, he says that to develop a normal, healthy child into a drug addict or alcoholic, parents must do several things:

1. Spoil him; give him everything he wants.
2. When he does wrong, nag him but never spank him.
3. Foster his dependence on you so that drugs or alcohol can replace you when he is older.
4. Make all his decisions for him since you are older and wiser than he is: he might make mistakes and learn from them if you don't.
5. Always bail him out of trouble so he will like you. Never let him suffer the consequences of his own behavior.
6. And just to play it safe, be sure that the mother dominates her husband and drives him to drink too, if she can.

There are many more items in this category, along with other categories such as the homosexual, the criminal, and the schizophrenic, but you begin to get the picture. In view of this it's easy to see how we have come to have a society that is full of these kinds of people. They're coming from homes where parents are not responding to the divine principles that lead a family into the will and purposes of God. No wonder a great number of parents say if they had it to do over they wouldn't have any children. After all, who wants children with problems like these?

But, there is one thing we can be grateful for, and that is this world does not have the last word on raising children -- God does. He has given us an effective and timeless piece of parental wisdom in Ephesians chapter 6 verses 1-4. We have already considered verses 1-3, directed to children. In verse 4 Paul is speaking to parents. *"And, father, do not provoke your children to wrath (anger); but bring them up in the training (discipline) and admonition (instruction) of the Lord."* Parents are to lead, but in a loving, spiritual way that does not abuse their children. The Greek word *"pateres"* used here for fathers means both father and mother. We have an example of this in Hebrews chapter 11 verse 23 when *"by faith Moses, when he was born, was hidden for three months by his parent* (pateres)...

So Paul is telling parents, you cannot just leave a child to develop on his/her own. You are the key to his/her life. Chaos will continue to destroy unless an environment of loving discipline breaks it. Children must be cared for. They are mentally, physically, spiritually, and socially inadequate to care for themselves. They need to grow in wisdom, in stature, and in favor with God and men."

David Walters in his book *"Children Aflame"* warns parents not to be content with just raising "good" children. He says, "we must seek to raise godly, anointed ones who know their God," he continues, "it is so easy to be content with your children having a form of godliness, but denying its power" (10) (Second Timothy 3:5).

Dr. Paul Meier, in his book we referred to earlier, says there are at least five keys to the right kind of parent-child relations:

- The first is LOVE. Parents must have genuine love for each other and for their children.

- The second is DISCIPLINE. A firm, consistent discipline is necessary.

- Third is CONSISTENCY. Both parents should use the same rules and consistently enforce them, so that what a child gets away with on some occasions, he is not being punished for on others.

- The forth key is EXAMPLE. As parents we must be the example for our children. We cannot expect them to live up to standards that we as parents don't maintain.

- Finally, it is important that there be HEADSHIP. Dr. Meier is echoing the biblical standard referring to the father as the head of the home. Research shows that a majority of neurotics grew up in homes where the father was either absent or weak and the mother was domineering. Both parents must be functioning in their proper roles to ensure success in fulfilling God's pattern for the raising of children.

The first role I want to talk about in the raising of children is the role of the mother. In many parts of the world today, especially America, very few mothers are at home. So who's raising the children and taking care of the home? In many cases, no one! I'm not attacking career-minded mothers because for most families to live above the poverty level it takes two incomes. But, I do believe many of the problems in our society are directly related to the absence of moms and dads being home. Let me add here that one of the reasons for moms having to work outside the home is fathers not properly preparing to fulfill their role as provider. I'll talk more about that later.

Many women will say, "I have a great job, and my family needs the money. How can God expect me to work at home?" Many mothers find it hard to understand why they should be expected to be at home raising the kids and not climbing the corporate latter and changing the world. And it's not the fault of moms today for having this attitude.

In most cases we have forgotten just how to change the world. It is changed best by those we raise up with the right values and morals. The one best suited to accomplishing this task and really change the world is mothers.

But let me take another view, a woman who works outside the home puts herself, most of the time, under authorities that have no biblical authority to be responsible for her as her husband is. Therefore she is changing her priorities that include areas that are not in line with God's divine order for wives and mothers.

Even this secular world is recognizing the negative results of wives and mothers leaving the home to take on a job or career. As stated by President George W. Bush in his speech at the 2004 Republican National Convention, two-thirds of mothers in America work outside the home today. Some writers say the troubles of children today are related to working mothers. Some writers even accuse working moms of undermining the husband's role, driving male wages down by increasing the supply of workers. It shatters the traditional American domestic life and the way of love and sex. Some have even said it brings an end to the lifetime, male-dominated, two-parent, multi-child, breadwinner family.

I realize that most people who hold these beliefs are being very hard on the working woman. And it started many years ago. But at some point we must stop and take a hard look at the result of children being raised in an environment where no one is home. I've spoken to numerous individuals that were raised in a home where

Marriage, Money and Romance

mom wasn't present very much and they're all seeking to go back and build that relationship in spite of whatever circumstance may exist.

We see it on television almost every day where children are seeking out their parents (predominately their mother). I've spoken to counselors from children's homes and they all say the children want nothing more than to be with their mothers no matter the abuse or neglect they may have suffered. Its time we start to change if we want a better future for our children and grandchildren.

There are a great number of wives and mothers that object and say, "I have a lot of energy and creativity and I want to do things." And that's great, but first please set your priorities and put things in God's order. Your first priority is always to God. You should have a devotion to knowing and living out His will according to His Word as stated in the following verses:

Col 3:16, *"Let the word of Christ dwell in you richly as you teach and admonish one another with all wisdom, and as you sing psalms, hymns and spiritual songs with gratitude in your hearts to God."*

1 Tim 2:15, *"But women will be saved through childbearing – if they continue in faith, love and holiness with propriety."*

Also a woman should have a dedication to walking in and by the Spirit so that the "fruit of the Spirit" is consistently manifested in her life as stated in these verses:

75

Eph 5:18, *"...be filled with the Spirit."*

Gal 5:16, *"So I say, live by the Spirit, and you will not gratify the desires of the sinful nature."*

Gal 5:22-23, *"But the fruit of the Spirit is love, joy, peace, patience, kindness, goodness, faithfulness, gentleness and self control..."*

Your second priority should be to your family. A wife and mother should be characterized by an unselfish devotion to her husband, children, and home; subjecting herself to her own husband -- seeing to his desires and needs over those of any other man, and raising godly children. Also she is to return provision and care to her parents. The lack of which is why we have a nursing home industry to take that responsibility for us.

Titus 2:5, *"To be self-controlled and pure, to be busy at home, to be kind, and to be subject to their husbands, so that no one will malign the word of God."*

Col 3:18, *"Wives, submit to your husbands, as is fitting in the Lord."*

Eph 5:22-23, *"Wives, submit to your husbands as to the Lord. For the husband is the head of the wife as Christ is the head of the Church, his body, of which he is the Savior."*

Eph 6:1-4, *"Children, obey your parents in the Lord, for this is right. Honor your father and mother which is the first commandment with a promise – that it may go well with you and that you may enjoy long life on the earth. Father, do not exasperate your children; instead, bring them up in the training and instruction of the Lord."*

1 Tim 5:4, *"But if a widow has children or grandchildren, these should learn first of all to put their religion into practice by caring for their own family and so repaying their parents and grandparents for this is pleasing to God."*

And finally women should be concerned with fellow saints. She should be a teacher and disciple the younger generation which includes devotion to instruction and to being an example of biblical teaching in regard to the priorities of husband and family. She is to be doing good works, which include being hospitable, serving fellow saints, and caring for orphans, widows, and those in distress.

Titus 2:4, *"..train the younger women to love their husbands and children..."*

1 Tim 2:10, *"but with good deeds, appropriate for women who profess to worship God."*

The next role I want to discuss is the father. A father is to be the head of the family. Total responsibility lies with him. He is to provide protection, provision, and spiritual growth to his family. We have far too many absentee fathers or fathers who take no responsibility for providing love and discipline in the home. The guidelines set by God are very clear.

> Eph 5:25-29, *"Husbands, love your wives, just as Christ loved the Church and gave himself up for her to make her holy, cleansing her by the washing with water through the word, and to present her to himself as a radiant church, without stain or wrinkle or any other blemish, but holy and blameless."*

I'll say it again, too many homes today have no father or a father with no authority. There are many causes for this but I want only to look at the results. Children need a father figure as an example: for girls to know what to look for in a husband; for boys to know how to love, care for, and protect the woman they take as a wife.

Many studies state that fathers spend very little time with their children at a time they are most vulnerable, just before going to bed. In fact families spend too little time together each day, and many experts feel here is the root of the problem today—TIME. And I'm not talking about quality, I'm talking about quantity. Children need your attention; they want only to know that you care about them. And one of the best ways to show our love is with our time and attention.

Fathers, you need to follow the instructions God gave in the Bible. Do not provoke them to anger, but bring them up in the discipline and instruction of the Lord. Love them, discipline them, and teach them. Instruct them in every area so they will grow to be pleasing in the sight of God and man. The best way to bring up children is by being the example for them to follow.

One father summed it up practically in this way: "My family is all grown, the kids are all gone, but if I had to do it all over, this is what I would do:

> I would love my wife more in front of my children.
> I would laugh with my children more – at our mistakes and our joys.
> I would listen more – even to the youngest child.
> I would be more honest about my own weaknesses and stop pretending perfection.
> I would pray differently for my family: instead of focusing on them I would focus more on me.
> I would do more things with my children
> I would do more encouraging and bestow more praise.
> I would pay more attention to little things, deeds, and words of love and kindness.
> Finally, if I had to do it again, I would share God more intimately with my family. I would use every ordinary thing that happened in every ordinary day to point them to God.

I hope every father reading this chapter will recognize what needs to be done, and if it isn't happening now make some changes so you will not have to look back when your children are grown and say "I should have, I wish I had, or If I could have." Start now to be the example, it's never too late.

Begin to mentor your son's so they will understand how to plan for marriage and how to love, provide for, and protect the one they choose for a life partner. Show your daughters what to look for in a husband, be the example in loving their mother. Let them see how a husband should treat his wife, how he should love her and care for her.

God wants our families to reach their full potential and not be forced into the mold of this world. God desires that Christian families not fall apart. Wouldn't it be great if we had children who were happy, homes that were Christ-centered where all these things were functioning as God designed them? It is possible because God promises it! And when it really begins to happen, the world will take notice of us...and of our Christ. Let it start with you!

Answer the questions below and share them with your family. By doing so it will help each of you improve your relationship and develop habits that will strengthen your love and unity.

1. How can I be more of a positive example to my children?

   _____

   _____

   _____

2. What are the top 3 things my children need, excluding material needs?

   _____

   _____

   _____

3. How can I communicate more with my children?

   _____

   _____

   _____

4. How do I discipline my children and what guidelines do I set for them?

_____

_____

_____

5. What activities can we do to increase our time together?

_____

_____

_____

5

Does our house have room for an extra person?

The secret of a good family life is simply to cultivate the family's relationship with Jesus. It should start with divine order in the home, but divine order by itself is not enough. As God's order begins to mold and fashion the outward form of a family's life, the presence of Jesus must be acknowledged fully to transform its inner life.

If the truth were known, adults today would confess the same confusion and frustration expressed by many children. They know about Jesus and they truly believe in Him, yet the experience of a distinct personal relationship is unclear or non-existent. A personal relationship implies a definite encounter and exchange between you and Jesus. If my wife and I have a long talk over the dinner table, we do not come away from the table wondering whether we have spoken with one another. We are not bothered with uncertainty as to whether there actually has been a personal encounter or not. Yet for many Christians the sense of a personal relationship with Jesus is uncertain or unclear.

We were traveling in Germany a few years ago, and we needed directions to a certain location we were trying to find. I saw a Shell Gas Station and I recognized it because it looked exactly like all the Shell Stations in America. I stopped and went in to ask directions and when I came back to the car my wife asked, "What did they say?" I simply replied, "They can't talk." What I meant was they can't speak English and I can't understand German. This is the experience of many Christians. The outward symbols of personal relationship—words like "see," "speak," and "know" are familiar but when people try to enter into the experience of these words in another realm, the realm of the Spirit, they become disappointed and frustrated.

To draw out the point of the illustration: A person who is a Shell station attendant in Germany does not always speak English for the simple reason that English is not the primary language in Germany. The Lord does not communicate with us like a human-person for the reason that He is a Spirit-Person.

In trying to convey to our children the understanding of a personal God, we have given far too little attention to this simple fact. Jesus said, *"God is Spirit, and those who worship Him must worship in spirit and truth"* (John 4:24). He has revealed Himself to us as Father, Son and Holy Spirit. We must keep in mind the fact that this relationship is with a Spirit-Person. We must communicate in the spirit realm. We must know Him if we are to be successful.

How do we know God? Study His Word and pray daily. The more you get into His presence through the word and through prayer, the more you'll begin to understand that communication is easy once you get into the spirit realm. But you must learn to get there if you want to hear and grow in the things of God. I couldn't speak to the German attendant because I hadn't studied the language, and it's the same with communicating to God. We must study and learn His personality and character in order to know him and hear Him.

It has been said that God saves families, and there is biblical truth that backs this up. The first is in Genesis chapter 7 verse 1. This is where we find Noah who constructed an ark for the saving of his household. There is much we can learn from Noah and the ark to help us today. I encourage you to study it closely. In Acts chapter 16 verse 31 we also see the jailer in Philippi who was saved, together with his household. In Exodus chapter 12 verse 3 we find the Passover – the great type of salvation. Deliverance in the Old Testament stipulated "a lamb for a household." We should take seriously these biblical types, and claim our households for God. Jesus was the lamb for us.

This is the beginning point for Christian family living. Each family member, at their own level of understanding, needs to experience the forgiveness which God offers us through Christ Jesus. Each must know Jesus as the Savior of the family.

Donny Ingram

As parents we should start teaching our children Christ at birth. The Bible leaves no doubt that young children can even enter into a personal experience with Jesus. In Matthew chapter 18 verse 6 Jesus spoke of a child as *"one of these little ones who believe in me."* In Mark chapter 9 verse 36 we can see another parallel passage that indicates the child was still small enough to be held in Jesus' arms. Even Paul when he addressed the saints in Ephesus and Colosse, clearly included the children.

John the Baptist had a clear-cut response to the Lord Jesus before either he or Jesus was born! The scripture tells us that when Elizabeth heard the greeting of Mary, the babe leaped in her womb. She exclaimed, *"when the voice of your greeting came to my ears, the babe in my womb leaped for joy"* (Luke 1:44). We must convey Christ to our children from the very start and continually help them in building a relationship, not just a learned doctrine, with Jesus Christ. Our children must see God answer their prayers and experience His intervention in their situations and meet their needs.

A child whose faith consists solely of a learned doctrine may have that faith badly shaken when it collides with rival doctrines in school, college or the workplace. But a child who carries within him the memory of countless encounters with the reality of God will not have to worry about holding his faith, his faith will hold him.

As parents, too often we fail to lead our children into simple ventures of faith. I believe we don't because parents themselves are afraid to lay their own faith on the line. We

86

have the fear, "What if nothing happens?" Well, what if nothing does happen? If God is not a prayer-answering God, aren't we better off to find it out now, and be done with this nonsense? If God can't be approached with our everyday needs, aren't we better off to discover it right now, so that our children can be spared the hypocrisy of believing in an all-powerful God who never lifts a finger?

Charlotte and I wanted our sons to experience God for themselves. We wanted them to encounter God on their level and grow up being able to understand the things of God and expect Him to answer their prayers and provide for their needs. I think we were successful because each of them seemingly has unshakable faith. All three have experienced God working in their lives to teach them, open doors for them, and provide for their every need. They understand that giving to God opens the door to receiving His blessing. I've seen each of them give every dime in his pocket to meet a need for someone that God placed on his heart.

* * *

Unanswered prayer is like an unsuccessful experiment – a reason to continue or further our research.

* * *

All three of our sons will tell you the scholarships they received to attend college came from God. Josh confesses that God provided his apartment while away at college.

The apartment complex where he wanted to live didn't allow college students, but they made an exception and allowed him to live there. He says God furnished every room of his apartment because he prayed, believed, and expected. They're grown now and their faith is stronger than ever. All three are working to help others recognize and follow the principles that work. Don't misunderstand, all of us still struggle at times, we face tragedy, sickness, hurt, and pain. The difference is we already know the outcome because we know who's in control – God. Why? Because we give Him control.

I read an article once where a professor sacrificed his standing as a scientist when he refused to carry out an experiment involving a given element because of fear his students might lose faith in that element. If he had experimented freely and openly he could have led his students into a precise and confident knowledge of just how the element reacts under varying conditions.

We should teach our children to understand that oftentimes prayers are un-answered for a while or the answer is no or wait. At other times it's just silence, as though God isn't even listening to our prayers. We must have the courage to venture with our children into these waters that test our faith. It is here that we learn how to pray. It is here that we wrestle with God until He blesses us. It is here that the encounter with God becomes real. Unanswered prayer is like an unsuccessful experiment – a reason to continue or further our research.

As a family experiences Jesus as Savior, their commitment to Him as Lord becomes stronger. Jesus should not occupy the guest room in your home, but the throne room. Every discussion, activity and decision should have as its foundation the fact that this thing involves not only family members, but also involves Jesus – He is our Lord.

Two aspects of family life serve as helpful keys opening the way for Jesus to exercise His Lordship over our family's lives and activity. They involve a commitment of two basic ingredients of our lives: Time and Money!

Time means a set time each day for family worship. It is necessary to make a specific commitment of time for this purpose. If Jesus is truly alive, if He is truly the Lord of our families, then it is unthinkable that a period of time should not be set aside each day exclusively for Him. Families discover sometimes with great surprise that a simple thing as time for family worship has such a transforming effect on everything that happens within the home. The reason is not hard to find.

When you commit time to anything at all, you set up a reaction situation between yourself and that to which you commit yourself. You commit time to eating breakfast: your body acts upon the food you eat, and the food has an inevitable effect upon your body. You take time to telephone a friend and make an appointment for lunch: your day is affected, his schedule is affected, the day of the parking attendant, the waitress, the cooks at the restaurant are all affected to the extent of your visit. When a family commits significant time exclusively to Jesus, they set up a reaction situation between themselves and Him, the Lord of heaven and earth. They open the door to all the creative potential which Jesus would bring into that family.

The second basic commitment of the family is money. Money means at least one-tenth of the family income given to the Lord. Money, as one man said, is congealed sweat. It is an affidavit of the time and skill we have to put out, which gives us claim on certain material necessities.

When a family commits the first tenth of its income to the Lord, it links its material destiny to God. The Bible clearly speaks of the tithe as an investment. *"Bring all the tithes in...and prove me now in this, says the Lord of hosts, if I will not open for you the windows of heaven and pour out for you such blessing..."* (Malachi 3:10). When God asks for the tithe, He invites a family to set aside fear and greed and let Him have the first tenth of its income. He promises, in return, to bless them materially. And, time and time and time again families who have trusted Him have learned that He is so able to bless their labor, so able to protect them from unnecessary outlays that they experience no lack.

This has been true in our personal life. God has never failed to supply all our needs and He promises He never will as long as I commit everything to him especially my time and my money. These two things are essential to showing that He is truly Lord of our life.

Romans chapter 10, verse 9 says we must make him Lord and lord means owner. If I'm living in a house that belongs to someone else that person is known as the landlord. I call the landlord when something breaks or something is needed for the house. When we make Jesus the Lord of our life we're making him owner of all we have and all we will ever have. Therefore, giving it to Him should be easy once we have made him Lord.

Tithing has so often been presented as a solemn duty that we have missed its deeper significance: God wants to bless us in material possessions. He wants a family to know security at this point. But He wants the security to be rooted in Him, not in a job or in a comfortable accumulation of assets. The family which learns to trust the Lord in this point experiences a security that no portfolio of stocks and bonds can match. These two basic commitments of time and money establish a foundation for the Lordship of Christ in a family. They tie us to Jesus. I want to continue in the next chapter to expound on what God has to say about our money.

The questions below will help you identify and plan ways to make the changes necessary to give Jesus priority in your life and home.

1. Do we attend church where we can receive instruction on the principles of God? If not what can we do to change?

   _____

   _____

   _____

2. How many times in the past month have I prayed to God and how long?

   _____

   _____

   _____

3. What can I do to help my family grow closer to God?

   _____

   _____

   _____

4. What things or situations are we facing that I should pray for?

_____

_____

_____

5. What can I do to set aside more time for Jesus?

_____

_____

_____

6

What does Money Have to do with Anything?

The one area that seems most difficult to get a grip on in life is finances. Most all the couples I've spoken with over the last thirty years in addition to Charlotte and I, have faced financial problems. Even though other areas are equally important I believe money is the one area that is troubling to all married couples, young and old, Christian and non-Christian. I guess that's why so many people misquote scripture and say that money is the root of all evil. But that's not exactly what the Bible says. It is the *"love"* of money that is the root of all evil. Therefore we need to understand that money isn't bad; it's when we put our trust in money and not in God that we get in trouble. However, divine help has already been made available in God's Word for the person who has a relationship with Jesus Christ.

*   *   *

God has a structured method to meet the needs in every area of our life

*   *   *

I want to provide some insight and understanding from a Christian prospective on God's principles in the area of finances, specifically in the area of giving. I realize we need to know about budgeting, spending habits and saving, but there are many books and seminars on these topics. God has a structured method to meet the needs in every area of our life, and the one that is most beneficial is giving. I want to focus on giving because this is the area that most know nothing about, and I believe it is the one area that can open the door to living a fruitful life.

Unlike the world's method of investing in stocks, bonds, mutual funds, and savings, along with stepping on others to climb to the top, God's method of multiplying our resources is stated in Luke chapter 6 verse 38, *"give and it shall be given to you, good measure, pressed down, shaken together and running over..."* As my father once told me "it's not how much you make, it's how you manage what you make." I have found this to be very true. However, if I fail to follow God's principles of giving, managing finances will be even more difficult because the enemy of our soul is out to "kill, steal, and destroy" us. One way he has been successful in accomplishing this is through our money and keeping us in lack, debt and fear.

The only sure way we can protect our finances and see them grow is through the Biblical principles of giving. Don't get me wrong, we must be good stewards and be wise about earning, spending, and saving. But the one area we need to learn more about and become more disciplined in is giving.

The subject of giving to God has caused more controversy in the Christian community today than any other single subject. I'm sure that's why Jesus talked more about finances than he did about anything else, even prayer. If my calculations are correct there are over 2300 scriptures referring to money and possessions. Jesus even called money his greatest competitor in Matthew chapter 6 verse 24, *"You cannot serve both God and money."* When He stood in the temple for the first time to address the congregation he spoke to the "poor" first. He said in Luke chapter 4 verse 18, *"...because he hath anointed me to preach the gospel (good news-NIV) to the poor..."* What is good news to a poor person? They don't have to be poor any longer! Jesus came to make us free. Free from the bondages of debt, sickness, poverty and everything that the enemy uses to hold us back or stop us from becoming what God planned from the very beginning.

I've heard many speakers talk about money and some had a "name-it-frame-it-claim-it" message. I believe this type of message turned many people away from believing that God has provided *"more than enough"* for everyone in His family. I believe the scriptures confirm that God meant for each of us to *"prosper in all things and be in health..."* as 3 John verse 2 says. He gives us a clue as to how it will work in this same verse, *"just as your soul prospers."* We can expect to prosper financially as we grow in our relationship with Jesus and trust Him with our life and future. We must be as the Bible states in the book of James, *"...a doer of the word and not hearers only, deceiving your own selves."*

In studying the scriptures through the years and listening to great men and women of God who received revelation from the Word, I have come to realize there are seven specific types of giving according to the Bible. They are: tithing, offerings, first-fruits, missions, alms, giving to the man and woman of God, and sowing for increase. Each area is important, especially for the Christian who needs to prosper financially. Without prospering we can't bless others, and that's God's purpose according to what He told Abraham in Genesis chapter 12 verse 2 *"I will make you a great nation and I will bless you and make your name great and you shall be a blessing."* We are Abraham's seed as Galatians chapter 3 verse 29 states, *"And if you are Christ's, then you are Abraham's seed, and heirs according to the promise."* As I discuss each area of giving please allow the Holy Spirit to guide you as the Word promises, *"in all Truth"* because He is the *"Spirit of Truth."*

Tithing

The first area of giving to examine is tithing which is commanded by God as a tenth of every dollar that comes into our possession. Some people say that tithing is an Old Testament doctrine, but let me start by giving you a simple truth that will help you in studying the Bible. All the teachings and doctrines of the Old Testament are filtered through the cross. As this is done one of three things will happen. They will be altered or changed, they will be eliminated, or they will pass through intact.

We have ample evidence of this in the writings of Paul in particular. Paul deals with the kosher laws of cooking and eating at length. The restriction against eating certain food taught in the Old Testament is all but eliminated in the New Testament. The final word on this is found in Acts chapter 15 verse 20.   This shows us that these laws were filtered through the cross and greatly changed.

The doctrine of circumcision was an absolute necessity and religious rite in the Old Testament times but survives in the New Testament primarily as a sanitary measure. The observances of certain days were required in the Old Testament but we are free from the obligation to observe them today. God has gone to great lengths in the New Testament to be sure that we know what things have been changed as a result of Calvary and what things have not.

Murder is hardly mentioned in the New Testament, so Old Testament laws concerning it are unchanged. Stealing is not dealt with in the New Testament therefore the Old Testament laws remain intact. The same is true of tithing. Tithing is hardly mentioned in the New Testament, so we can safely say God still demands that we bring away to Him the hallowed things (the tithe) and observe His law concerning them.

In fact many think tithing was under the Old Testament law and now that we're under grace we're not required to tithe. However, we find in Genesis chapter 14 that Abraham was paying tithes some 400 years before the law was even given. Therefore all the law did was give tithing a structure and make it a requirement. It was always a principle of God and His principles never change. Therefore, we must tithe today.

Hebrews chapter 8 verse 6 says, *"We have a better covenant established upon better promises."* The New Testament made the Old Testament stronger with more power and freedom for us to live by today. Isaiah and Solomon also gave us some insight as to how to follow the guidelines of God's Word. In Ecclesiastes chapter 1 verses 9-10 He said, *"The thing that hath been, it is that which shall be; and that which is done is that which shall be done: and there is no new thing under the sun. Is there anything whereof it may be said, See, this is new? It hath been already of old time, which was before us"* and Isaiah 46:9-10 says, *"Remember the former things of old: for I am God, and there is none else; I am God, and there is none like me, declaring the end from the beginning, and from ancient times the things that are not yet done, saying, My counsel shall stand, and I will do all my pleasure."(KJV)* Therefore if we want to know how to walk, talk, live and give today we must go back to the beginning to see how God originally planned it. So let's go back to the place we find the first account of someone paying tithe in Genesis chapter 14 verses 18-20 and then we'll follow it to Hebrews chapter 7 verses 1-4.

Genesis chapter 14 verses 18-20 states, *"Then Melchizedek King of Salem brought out bread and wine; he was the priest of the God most high. And he blessed him, and said, blessed be Abram of God most high, possessor of heaven and earth: And blessed be God most high, who has delivered your enemies into your hand. And he (Abram) gave him tithe of all."*

Hebrews chapter 7 verses 1-4 says, *"For this Melchizedek, king of Salem, priest of the most high God, who met Abraham returning from the slaughter of the kings, and blessed him..."* It is important to note what had been going on in Abraham's life when we see him in these scriptures. He was returning from what the Bible calls the "slaughter of the kings." These kings are the five kings of the land of Palestine. Something else we should notice is that Abraham had not only taken 318 men and conquered all the army's of Palestine, but he had taken great spoils. Spoiled to us today means unfit for consumption. But here it means "bounty". He defeated the five kings and had taken all that they possessed. We have a New Testament picture of Jesus doing this in Colossians chapter 2 verse 15, *"And having spoiled principalities and powers, he made a show of them openly, triumphing over them in it."*

Satan is pictured in the Bible as the god of this world. When Jesus arose from the dead, He took the only thing satan had that was of value. He took possession of the souls that had been held captive. Jesus also took back Adam's dominion that had been forfeited to Satan when Adam sinned in the Garden. He took back the keys to death and hell. Jesus left him totally bankrupt. He did it so you and I could live more abundantly and once again have dominion over the things of this world.

As a matter of fact Jesus gave us a promise in Matthew chapter 19 verse 29, *"And every one that has left houses, or brethren, or sisters, or father, or mother, or wife, or children, or lands, for my name's sake, shall receive an hundredfold and inherit everlasting life."* The books of Mark and Luke both say we will receive a hundredfold now in this present time. But we must follow Abraham's example and go after it, and once God has given us the victory use it according to His plan.

Abraham was coming up from the slaughter of the kings and he probably had a smile on his face and a song in his heart. He was victorious. He then went to someone that many believe to be Jesus in the Old Testament. For sure he was a type of Christ, if not Christ himself – *"Melchizedek."* Let's look at his titles: first he is called the King of Righteousness, and second he is referred to as the King of Salem, which is peace. This is important because there can be no peace without first being in right-standing with God.

The whole world is looking for peace. Everyone wants peace in their marriages and family relationships. You'll never have peace in your marriage without observing God's laws of love and submission. You'll never have peace in relationships until God is in them, and God will only show up if things are done His way. You'll never have peace in church until things are done God's way. There's never peace in your finances until God invades them, and

He will only come on His terms. Lamentations chapter 3 verse 17 tells us one of the reasons we don't have peace is because we have forgotten what prosperity is all about. God prospers us so we can be a blessing to others.

Most people want to win by default. They think they'll win just because they show up on Sunday morning and Sunday night, that is if they haven't had a bad Saturday and there's something they really want to see or hear. They might even attend Wednesday night if their calendar is absolutely clear. As a result of our "faithfulness" to show up, we think all the spoil of the kingdom is supposed to be ours. It doesn't work that way. Abraham had to go after it. You don't win just by showing up. He not only went but he conquered, he took the spoil, he tasted the honey, and he enjoyed victory. After he won, the next step was to obey God rather than man. Abraham had a prime opportunity to fail.

Many times in my life I failed due to ignorance of God's Word and His divine purpose for my family. For years I never used a budget, never had a disciplined savings plan, and I made poor financial decisions that hindered us for the long term. Only once did I not give God ten percent of my income. We had been married for about a year and I decided that we needed that money to pay bills instead of paying tithe one month. Before the month was out our car broke down and it cost me exactly what I would have given in tithe. Now some would call this a coincidence, but I believe a coincidence is just an event where God chooses not to reveal himself. I repented and never again withheld my tithe from God. And God has remained true to His Word and his promises throughout our life.

As Abraham came to this priest of God, he dealt with God's claims on his life. Verse 2 says, *"To whom also Abraham gave a tenth part of all,"* not a tenth of some, but all. Abraham gave to God a tenth of everything even though he wasn't going to keep any of it. There is a principle here that we need to grab on to and that is all we possess, even if it is for a short while, we must give God a tenth. In my years of serving in several churches I have held the position of clerk, or as some call it, the financial administrator. While serving in this position I witnessed first hand that very few members paid exactly ten percent or more. Many gave a few dollars each week or month and thought God should bless everything they had and everything they did. One research group reported that only six percent of born again adults tithed in 2002. This represents an eight percent decline from 2001 and a six percent decline from 2000.*(11)* No wonder so many people are having trouble spiritually, physically, emotionally and financially.

Malachi instructs us also to give God tithe (10 %) of all we gain. Malachi asks the question, *"Will a man rob God? Yet you rob me. But you ask, "how do we rob you? In tithes and offerings."* He even says in verse 9 that because of this *"You are under a curse..."* He goes on in verse 10 to say, *"Bring the whole tithe into the storehouse, that there may be food in my house."* He even says *"prove me (test me) in this, and see if I will not throw open the floodgates of heaven and pour out so much blessing that you will not have room enough for it."* I urge you to prove God and give Him a tenth of every payday and see what He will do for you. For over thirty years Charlotte and I have lived by this principle and God has never failed to bless and protect our income.

Tithing will protect your resources from the enemy. That's why Malachi goes on to say in verse 11, *"I will rebuke the devourer for your sakes, so that he will not destroy the fruit of your ground..."* God is obligated to protect your possessions when you are dedicated to tithing. He will never fail!

Several years ago we were in serious financial difficulty because of bad decisions on my part. During that time we never failed to pay tithe on every nickel we made. In that time of need God moved on several people to give us money. Don't misunderstand me, we didn't go begging or poor-mouthing as I've heard some do. I believe if you're doing what God has outlined you to do he will supply all your needs just by asking Him. As far as anyone else could see we were having no problems.

Charlotte and I, as well as the boys, prayed and asked God for help. It wasn't long until God answered our request. One lady stopped us in the parking lot and handed us a $500 check. She said God told her to bless us. Another lady invited Charlotte to lunch and gave her a check for $1000 dollars. She said, "I don't know why God wanted me to give this to you. As far as I know you guys are doing great, but I must obey Him."

Offerings

The second area of giving I want to discuss is offerings. Throughout scripture we find God requiring offerings from his people. In the Old Testament we see grain offerings, wheat offerings, fellowship offerings, sin offerings, etc. Malachi addresses offerings at the same time he addresses tithing. We can even go to Luke chapter 21 verses 3 and see offerings being given and Jesus' response to the widow that gave. *"...Truly I say to you that this poor widow has put in more than all..."* We give offerings to meet needs, bless others, construct buildings, and a multitude of other things which in turn blesses God. God is a giver as John chapter 3 verse 16 says, *"for God so loved the world, that He gave..."* He gave His best, *his only son, that whosoever believeth in him should not perish, but have everlasting life."* God will never ask us to do something He has not done Himself.

Giving offerings helps us tear down the walls built by the enemy. If you study the history of the kings of Israel you'll find only a few followed after God. But those that did began their reign by doing something that I believe directly relates to our finances today. They destroyed the idols placed on the high places and gave the high places back to God. An idol we put on our high places today is money and the things it can purchase. We must tear down the high places in our lives and give them back to God. I'm not saying that God wants us to give every dollar we get to a church or to those in need. God wants us to prepare for a rainy day, have a savings account, and invest in our future with stocks, mutual funds and 401ks. But we must put our priorities in order.

God provided four streams in the garden to feed the garden and Adam and Eve. I believe God wants you and me to have at least four streams of income in our lives to feed and meet our needs and the needs of others that God places in our path. Most of us have four streams already. We just haven't developed them to the point where they are providing what we want them to pay. Most of us have some sort of savings, retirement account (personal or company), investments (stocks, bonds, mutual funds or real estate) and some of us have discovered that God has placed gifts, talents and skills in us that can, if we develop and use them, produce income. I heard of one lady that received so many compliments on how beautiful her hands were that she had them photographed and now is using them to advertise jewelry exclusively for one company. My point is, figure out what God has placed in you and use it to your benefit and His Kingdom.

As I've already stated, God's Word promises us in Luke chapter 6 verse 38, *"Give, and it will be given to you; good measure, pressed down, and shaken together, and running over, will be put into your bosom..."* The logic is that we can't receive until we give. Some call this a cause and effect principle, others a mutual benefit principle, but I call it an action and response principle. When you take action to give, you set in motion a response from God. This same verse goes on to tell us that very fact. *"...For with the same measure that you use, it will be measured back to you."* So how will you measure up?

First Fruits

The third area of giving is first fruits. In Exodus, Leviticus and Deuteronomy we find God instructing the Israelites to bring their first fruits to God. The first fruits are to be given to ensure a continual increase in your income. Proverbs chapter 3 verses 9-10 confirm this very fact, *"Honor the Lord with your possessions, and with the first fruits of all your increase: So your barns will be filled with plenty, and your vats will overflow with new wine."* Romans chapter 11 verse 16 also says, *"if the first fruits be holy the lump is also holy..."* showing us again another way God protects our harvest because the devil can't touch that which is holy and blessed of God.

Churches abound today, but for the most part their people are powerless. When Christians practice, and churches condone, robbing God of first fruits, they'll always be powerless, just as Israel was at Ai. Their victory at Jericho was great, and the next town to conquer was Ai. It was small, and Joshua's reconnaissance reported that it would be easily defeated, not requiring more than 2000-3000 soldiers to take it. Not only could they not defeat Ai, but the men of that little city put Israel's army to flight and killed 36 of their men. Joshua was stunned. He immediately fell on his face and asked God why.

The first city they came to in this new promised land was Jericho. And God instructed them that nothing of Jericho was to be taken for personal possession but to be used for God. Jericho was a type of first fruits of the new land. It was the insurance that they would receive a blessing in that land. But the flesh got in the way.

Another thing we should remember about this part of history is when something fails we should go to God in prayer. Instead most want to study the problem and ask others what to do. We add another committee, or start another training session to beef up the numbers and advertise more. If only believers would genuinely repent and get right with God financially, then we would see miraculous things start to occur. If all of the resources that should have been given to God were removed from retirement plans, bank accounts, and investments and brought into God's house, there would be enough to do everything the church has been commanded to do. And those who gave it would be blessed above any interest that money would produce.

Joshua knew the only way to solve the problem was to go to God. God told him that Israel had sinned. *"They have transgressed my covenant which I commanded them: for they have even taken of the accursed (devoted) thing, and have also stolen, and dissembled also, and they have put it even among their own stuff."* In short they had sinned against God. They took the first fruits, which was devoted to God. Therefore, God's defense of them was removed. Because of this, Israel could not stand before their enemies. They didn't understand the problem at the time of the battle, fear gripped them and they tried to run away.

Adam and Eve experienced the same phenomenon. When they sinned and took that which was devoted to God, they became fearful. They ran away to hide. Proverbs chapter 28 verse 1 says, *"The wicked flee when no one pursues: but the righteous are bold as a lion."* God not only told Joshua the problem but also informed him that until the matter was dealt with He would no longer be with them.

Some scholars teach that the principle of first fruits is what caused God to accept Abel's offering and reject Cain's offering in Genesis chapter 4 verses 3-5. I've heard others teach that it was the amount that Abel brought, referring to the tithe. Whatever reason, tithe or first fruits, we don't have to make the same mistake. All we must do is obey in both.

First fruits are vital to our increase. We must begin to give God the first part of any increase we receive; raises, bonuses, promotions, inheritances, and gifts. Nowhere can I find that God set an amount for first fruits so the amount given is between you and God. Whatever you determine is right, do it. I've spoken with some who give their first pay check each year, and they say they're income increases every year. Others give on their increases each year, be it cost of living, bonuses, raises etc. The fact is, God will bless us when we acknowledge that He is the one in whom we place our trust and hope for the future.

Missions

The fourth area of giving is missions. If you've been in church and around Christians for any length of time you have probably heard Philippians chapter 4 verse 19 quoted. It says, *"my God shall supply all my needs according to his riches in glory according to Christ Jesus."* I use this scripture daily when I pray for my family to have all they need. But the one thing many fail to see is that the people who receive the promise of this scripture are those who give to missions. To understand that fact we must back up a few verses to verse 15 of Philippians chapter 4 which says, *"Now you Philippians know also, that in the beginning of the gospel when I departed from Macedonia, no church shared with me concerning giving and receiving, but you only. For even in Thessalonica you sent aid once and again for my necessities. Not that I seek the gift, but I seek the fruit that abounds to your account."* These are the people Paul was referring to when he wrote this promise.

Charlotte and I have always given to missions. I believe when Jesus gave us the command in Mark chapter 16 verse 15 *"to go into all the world"* he didn't mean that we all are to become full-time missionaries. However, by giving to missions you provide others the freedom to go and teach, go and build buildings, as well as to purchase books, clothes and food to be sent abroad. When you give to missions God's reward for you will be just as great as the one who physically goes to the mission field.

Mission giving is one of the most needed areas in ministry today. Without the giving to missions many would not have the opportunity to receive Jesus as Lord and Savior. We could not go *"into all the world"* as missionaries and do what Jesus commanded without resources. Spreading the gospel is expensive, and without committed Christians giving to missions many would be lost and God's plan hindered.

I praise God that America has developed and sent more missionaries and provided more money to evangelize the world than any other country. That's one reason our nation was raised up, and the main reason why we are so blessed as a country. However, more is needed today than ever before, and God's people must step up and answer the need.

Alms

The fifth area is Alms. Alms giving is giving to the poor and misfortunate. Proverbs chapter 28 verse 27 tells us, *"He who gives to the poor will not lack, but he who hides his eyes will have many curses."* I do not want to be cursed, but not wanting to be cursed is not why we should practice this principle. We should love everyone and have a desire to help others out of our love for people. This should be natural if we are born-again Christians because God lives in us and God is love. God loves the poor, homeless and misfortunate so much that He gave us a big promise if we would practice this principle. I'm so thankful that I'll never be in lack as long as I continue to give alms. Proverbs chapter 22 verse 16 also has a promise, *"He who oppresses the poor to increase his riches, and he who gives to the rich, will surely come to poverty."*

Proverbs chapter 19 verse 17 says, *"He that has pity on the poor lends to the Lord, and he will pay back what he has given."* When we give alms we are touching the heart of God because God loves everyone and desires to see no one suffer. One reason the first Gentile convert received an answer to his prayers from God was because he gave alms and prayed to God continually. Take a look at Acts chapter 10 verse 2, *"A devout (obedient) man, and one that feared God with all his household, who gave alms generously to the people, and prayed to God always."* And verse 4 says, *"Your prayers and your alms have come up for a memorial before God."* Would you like to have a memorial in heaven to remind God about you and your love for His creation? All we have to do is give alms.

God gives us some instruction on our alms giving in Matthew chapter 6 verses 1-4, *"Take heed that you do not do your charitable deeds (alms) before men, to be seen of them. Otherwise you have no reward from your Father in heaven. Therefore when you do a charitable deed (giving alms), do not sound a trumpet before you, as the hypocrites do in the synagogues and in the streets, that they may have glory from men. Assuredly, I say unto you, they have their reward. But when you do a charitable deed do not let your left hand know what thy right hand is doing, that your charitable deed may be in secret; and your Father who sees in secret will himself reward you openly."*

God is the only one that is to reward the alms giver. He sees all we do. Nothing takes him by surprise and as Ephesians chapter 6 verse 8 says, and I paraphrase, *"what you do for others God will do for you."* Many very successful people have made this their life's motto and because they live it, their blessings continue to increase. It is a principle of God and we should practice it faithfully.

In my travels I see many people standing on corners in the city with signs that read "will work for food" or "out of work, need help." It's hard for me not to give especially when God has given me so much. Once in Memphis Tennessee I was going to a meeting early one morning and on the off ramp of the highway stood a man with such a sign. Before I could get close to see what the sign said God spoke to my heart to give this man what I had in my pocket. I agreed until I got closer and saw that he was dressed very well; in fact his shoes looked better than mine. I began to question God and God's word to me was, *"I didn't ask you to judge him, I asked you to give him what you have in your pocket."* I did as God said and I felt much better. However, the story doesn't end there. After returning home I received a phone call from my boss that said the company had put something extra in my check that week to thank me for my hard work. The extra was $1,000 dollars.

Giving to the Man and Woman of God

The sixth area of giving is to the man and woman of God. First Timothy chapter 5 verses 17-18 says, *"Let the elders that rule well be counted worthy of double honor, especially they who labor in the word and doctrine. For the scripture says, you shall not muzzle an ox while it treads out the grain. And, the laborer is worthy of his wages."* I've witnessed many people disobeying this principle. There are ministries and teachers around the world working daily spreading the gospel of Jesus Christ and seeing great things happen in the lives of people, and they are depending on God to supply the resources to keep on working. God's way of blessing and supplying them is through people like you and me.

I have several friends that travel to preach and teach because of the call on their lives. Some churches barely give them enough gas money much less money to cover their bills and family needs. I'm so excited to be part of a body of believers that understand these principles of giving; especially giving to men and women whose full time occupation is ministering the gospel.

Our local church takes in hundreds of thousands annually and a great portion goes to missions every year. We are meeting the needs of widows, single parents and the poor every week with alms offerings. The men and women who come to minister at World Outreach Center are blessed beyond their wildest imagination. I've witnessed our people giving thousands of dollars to visiting ministers. And believe me, for a congregation of about 500, we have no big dollar millionaires, but we have a house full of givers and God is blessing our socks off.

The main reason for such a giving body is that we receive the Word continually on God's order for finances in our lives. Too many pastors are afraid to teach on giving because someone might get upset. If more would teach the principles of giving more people would be set free from the bondage of debt and be able to give more to the Kingdom of

God. We stand on the Word in Second Corinthians chapter 9 verses 6-14, *"...Whoever sows sparingly will also reap sparingly, and whoever sows generously will also reap generously..."* I'm not going to quote this entire chapter, but I would ask that you study it closely and determine in your heart what God would have you to do.

A few years ago I was on a mission trip to Uganda Africa with several teachers. We were teaching at a leadership conference for about a week. During this trip my friend gave his testimony about how God had supplied him with his own automobile business after he obeyed God and began to pay for one minister's cars. After hearing him I said to myself, "I sure wish I could be a giver like that." Immediately God said, "You can." I was startled but I replied, "No I can't, I don't have anything to give like that." And God replied, "You can give your home." I knew that wouldn't go over well with Charlotte.

We had moved up state about a year earlier and our house was just sitting there not being used because the couple who leased it moved out without notice. We were living in a rundown house that Charlotte's grandfather built in the early 1900's because the purchase of the home we had planned to buy fell through. Upon arriving back from my trip I told Charlotte what God had said and as you can imagine her reaction was less than favorable at first. But I left it to God to convince her because I knew she would consult God and make the right decision.

About three weeks later I was traveling in Louisiana and she called and said, "I know what we are to do with the house." She was excited and anxious at the same time. She had found out that a missionary family was returning from Kosovo where they had been ministering for eight years and had nowhere to go. I quickly agreed, and on my way back home I took the keys to the local pastor that knew the missionary family and informed him of what we wanted to do. He was quite surprised because he had never experienced anyone being that generous. That beautiful family of five lived in our home for seventeen months before God gave them another assignment.

By now you know that the story doesn't end there. At the same time we made the decision to give our home to this missionary family, God opened a door for my family to live in one of the most beautiful homes in the county. It had seven bedrooms, five baths and the wooded location was fabulous. And God took care of all the cost, even the utilities. I don't want to continue on because I don't want you to think we're something special because we're not. We're an average family that experiences the same struggles almost every family faces. We just try and follow God's guidelines in everything we do. But if God will do it for us He'll do it for you. Just believe!

Sowing for increase

After giving of tithe, offerings, first fruits, alms, giving to men and women who spread the gospel, you can then begin to sow your money for a return. This principle is where great increase begins to flow. The parable of the talents in Matthew chapter 25 verses 14-30 tell us this principle will work. *"Again, it will be like a man going on a journey, who called his servants and entrusted his property to them. To one he gave five talents of money, to another two talents, and to another one talent, each according to his ability."* (NIV) You can read the remainder of this parable and see that the harvest of the one that received five was doubled as well as the one that received two talents. However, the servant that received one talent did nothing with it, and therefore it was taken and given to another and he was cast into outer darkness.

There are a few things about this scripture I want you to see. First, why did they each receive different amounts? The scripture states it was according to their "ability." This word ability in Greek is "Dunamis" it means explosive energy, or more commonly defined as the power of God. This tells me they each received the amount based on their relationship with God. It says they were all servants or believers therefore they had a relationship with the master. But two obviously had greater relationships. The third moved in fear.

Verse 25 tells us he didn't do anything because he was afraid. How many people today are not using their talents or sowing their money because of fear? Fear is actually stopping people from being able to give and minister in the Kingdom of God. I like what my friend told me about fear. He said it is "False Evidence Appearing Real." How true! If we could only have faith we could see that God will never let us down. And if we're trying to obey His Word, even when we stumble and slip, slide and fall down, He's always present to help us up and get us on the right track again.

I would like to leave you with this verse of scripture in Galatians chapter 6 verses 7-10, *"Do not be deceived: God cannot be mocked. A man reaps what he sows. The one who sows to please his sinful nature, from that nature will reap destruction; the one who sows to please the Spirit, from the Spirit will reap eternal life. Let us not become weary in doing good, for at the proper time we will reap a harvest if we do not give up. Therefore, as we have opportunity, let us do good to all people, especially to those who belong to the family of believers."* NIV

When you sow your resources for God, tell Him what you're expecting in return. I had many people tell me that you're not supposed to expect anything in return. If that's so then why did God put it in His Word? I even name my seed when I sow my money into ministries and projects that God lays on my heart. If I plant apple seeds I don't expect to get grapes, therefore I tell God what I'm expecting in return according to what His Word says.

Let God speak to your heart about giving and become the giver He wants you to be. By doing so you will reap a harvest greater than you could ever imagine. Let me also give you this truth: I know that many people who begin giving to God biblically and immediately they start to have problems. Their car breaks, the washer/dryer quits, everything starts to cost money to fix. This is the enemy trying to show you that God's principles of giving aren't working. But don't stop short of receiving a blessing. It's like the Chinese bamboo tree. Once it's planted it must be watered and fertilized each year but no sign of any growth is seen until the fifth year. Sometime in the fifth year in a six-week period the tree grows to a height of around ninety feet. What would have happened if it received no water and fertilizer in the second, third, or forth Year? No ninety foot tree! The same is true with the Christian and giving. Don't stop! God can't lie. He said His word would do what He pleased; and He wants His children to prosper. That's His plan.

These seven ways of giving are working in the lives of many Christians today. My family has had numerous experiences of God blessing us financially, but I don't want to sound boastful. I'm no different than you or anyone else. If God has ever done it for one He'll do it for you because He is no respecter of persons. Study these scriptures, pray for direction, and let God begin to bless you to bless others.

Here are questions to help improve your actions in the area of giving. When you obey God's Word it causes the windows of heaven to open over you and shower blessings on every area of your life.

1. Do I give God 10% of my earnings? If not, how, when and where do I plan to start?

   _____

   _____

   _____

2. After paying tithes (10%) of my earnings what offerings can I begin to give and where?

First Fruits_____

Alms_____

Missions_____

Man & Woman of God_____

3. Where can I start sowing my money for increase?

   _____

   _____

   _____

7

What Happened to Romance and Intimacy

I've read many studies on marriage and divorce and I find that most of them point to two major problems, Sex and Money. When taking a closer look, I find that these problems are caused mainly from a single source – communication. Almost every article I've ever read on the marriage relationship referenced the failure of men being able to communicate effectively to their wives.

Without effective (honest, timely, & clear) communication we cannot know or understand each other; especially when it comes to what our mate's greatest needs are, what they want, or don't want, like or dislike, or when they like it, and when they don't like it. What would your spouse do if you looked him or her in the eye tonight and asked, "Sweetheart, what can I do to let you know that I love you?" Most wives would probably fall on the floor in shock. Most husbands would probably think that they're being manipulated so she can get something she wants.

One way we can improve our communication of love is to understand our spouse's love language. I highly recommend that every couple read Gary Chapman's book, *The Five Love Languages* and take the love language profile. I can truly say this resource has helped Charlotte and me tremendously and we use this love language profile every time we talk with couples experiencing problems. I even use it in teaching corporate sales seminars, because it shows how important it is that we find out how others think, and feel if we want to effectively meet their needs.

That's why some couples seem so head-over-heels in love with each other. It's not that their lives are any easier or more perfect than others – but they know what their spouses need to be shown in order to feel loved. And they know how to keep the daily grind from eroding their relationship by paying attention to the little things that is important to their spouse. They understand how to communicate love, and they practice honesty. Honesty is another major problem in marriage.

* * *

Our prayer closet is more important than the Oval Office, has more influence than the United Nations, and can accomplish more than all the dictators in the world combined

* * *

As God's Word is to us, our word should be to others especially our spouses. No lie can serve the purpose of God. There is no such thing as a "white lie." The closer the lie is to the truth, the more damning it is. All deceitfulness is a form of lying. Our own hearts, in their natural state, are deceptive. The only true way to know right from wrong is to have the Spirit of Truth born into us to witness the truth of our thoughts, words, motives and actions.

Before we communicate to others we need to have communication with God through prayer. Some of us call out to God and ask why this or that? Prayer is not used as some form of fire insurance to keep us out of trouble, or as a religious ritual. But genuine, authentic prayer is dealing with matters of heaven and hell based on the Word of God. I received an email from a friend a while back that said, "Our prayer closet is more important than the Oval Office, has more influence than the United Nations, and can accomplish more than all the dictators in the world combined."

I'm not going to dwell on the reason for or the benefits of prayer, we've already covered that, but I want to emphasize that it is a must. The Word says *"we have not because we ask not"* and we can only ask by prayer, but for our prayer to be unhindered we must be obedient to the Word.

We can't experience a fulfilled intimate relationship without good, clear, honest communication about what we think, want, and desire. Our communication must go farther than clichés, facts and opinions. We must communicate our true feelings and our needs if we expect to reach the ultimate level of intimacy. It is more difficult for us to share our feelings and needs because here is where we are most vulnerable, and offering up our deepest feelings is where we blow it many times.

* * *

A wife wants to be cuddled. She wants her husband to snuggle with her, hold her hand, and make her feel that she's the most valuable thing in the world

* * *

When we talk about intimacy most of us think sex. Sex is important! It's the highest physical act of love between two people to show their union in spirit, which is a covenant relationship. But intimacy is much more than sex, especially to a woman. According to a survey of over 100,000 women, those who had the deepest spiritual walk with God enjoyed a greater sex life with their husbands.

Men, your wives want to be complimented. They need to hear how much they mean to you. How much you appreciate them and who they are, as well as what they do. A wife wants to be cuddled. She wants her husband to snuggle with her, hold her hand, and make her feel that she's the most valuable thing in the world. The gift that God gave you! I've been known to turn the air conditioning down to fifty degrees in the summer and put a fire in the fireplace to get the atmosphere just right to cuddle with Charlotte, and let me tell you the rewards are wonderful.

Every wife wants to be kissed and not just on the lips but on the hand, on the neck, on the nose and on the cheek. There are tremendous benefits of kissing for husbands and wives. In a study completed by a large European insurance company, it was discovered that "men who get kisses from their wives before going to work and after arriving home (a kiss like a wife not a sister, and for most people I tell them this means a "wet-one") earn an average of twenty-five percent more income and lives five and one-half years longer than those that don't."(14) I believe that's reason enough to make a special effort to get that kiss, don't you?

*   *   *

Ladies your husbands are very simple characters. It doesn't take much to impress a husband. All a wife has to do is show up naked.

*   *   *

All wives want to be caressed, stroked, comforted, protected, hugged, and held because it communicates love. I never met a wife that didn't want her husband to spend money on her, take her out to dinner, listen to her, care for her and be there to support her. In short, a wife wants her husband to go to the ends of the earth for her. Some men might say that is asking too much! But in reality if you want her to respond to your needs just try it! It's called unselfishness! Put her needs before yours.

Ladies your husbands are very simple characters. It doesn't take much to impress a husband. All a wife has to do is show up naked. However, he also needs to know how much you appreciate him. He needs you to hold him up, encourage and strengthen him verbally. And of course, he needs to be nourished sexually and to be physically satisfied.

One thing I think is extremely important to remember for both the husband and wife is if you aren't meeting the needs of your mate there is always someone else who is willing to meet those needs. I know you don't want to think about this being a possibility but we see it taking place in too many marriages today. Opportunities will arise to lure you into the arms of another if you aren't prepared to resist. And resisting is harder for those who are not getting what they need from their spouses.

I travel almost every week, and several times the opportunity to commit adultery has surfaced. Being a very satisfied husband, and a strong Christian, I have very little problem resisting. I remember traveling to Nashville, Tennessee several years ago, and upon checking into my hotel I was approached by a young lady who asks if I needed some company for the evening. I quickly responded, "No thank you." But before I could get my suite case open the phone rang and another lady was asking me the same thing. I quickly realized I needed to change hotels and I moved down the road to another hotel.

The easiest way to keep from being faced with an opportunity to do wrong is to avoid putting yourself in a position where you are vulnerable. As a husband or wife we must strive to meet every need of our spouse, especially physically. By doing so we are doing our part in building a relationship on trust and honesty.

This brings me to an area many people fail to research and understand for themselves and that is sex - the act of physical intimacy. As we have already stated, men and women are different. We are made that way so we can complement and balance each other out. But I find in talking to men, every man wants to be significant to the love of his life, especially in their sex life. Men want the same things as women except they want to get there quicker and a woman wants intimacy to be in every part of her life.

When a man is intimate he is attentive to his wife's needs, he is sensitive to her emotions, and he is usually a patient listener. The big complaint from almost every wife is that her husband doesn't spend enough time being intimate. She is confused as to why her husband doesn't spend more time in pursuit of intimacy. For a marriage to stay in tune, fired up, exciting and inviting, intimacy must be an ongoing event.

Women want to be romanced continually. They don't want your attention only after the lights go out; they want it to start when the lights come on in the morning! I'll be honest, this isn't easy to get into the habit of doing but it can be fun once you get it started and start reaping the rewards. When a husband does the little things for his wife, like thanking her for doing the small things, kissing her neck or hand, opening the door, leaving her little gifts from time to time, planning a night out, making her feel like the special gift she is, she will become all he could expect and much more.

Let me relay some insight about why men are the way they are. According to research when men start to have sex on a regular basis, their bodies adjust to an anticipated schedule of intercourse. For example: If a couple is enjoying sexual pleasure every couple of days after they marry, say for the first several months of marriage, the man's body will become accustomed to that time table and expect it on that schedule. But as we all are aware, no couple ever stays "on schedule" and that is where the tension builds. The man's body still prepares for that release even if he knows intellectually it is not going to happen. Here is where the cruelty of sex shows up.

When he doesn't have the sexual release "on schedule" he begins to experiences a number of reactions physically and emotionally, such as pressure in his body. He finds himself staring at his wife more and more as her features intensify in his mind. The longer he stares the more he longs to be with her. As time goes on he may become irritable and even difficult to deal with. He loses sight of much of what is really great about his life. At the same time he knows the reality of what's happening. He's strong he understands that being married means being patient and he says to himself, "I can wait." But no amount of self-reasoning seems to reduce the tension he feels in his body. If the stress of his life is high this struggle will intensify." I wish more wives could understand what is happening at this moment in her husband's mind and body. If this continues it can hinder his decision making ability especially at home.

I was listening to the radio a few months ago during a business trip and they cited a recent study by Mayo Clinic that said sexual pleasure was a stress reliever. They said that sex also increases the level of estrogen for women as well as reduces cholesterol for men. I came home excited about my new found knowledge about how to help Charlotte increase her estrogen and reduce my cholesterol, and reduce our stress level but she wasn't as excited about the findings as much as I was. She wanted written proof of the study. I'm still trying to find the results of that study!

I'm reminded of something I was told at the last marriage retreat I attended. It seems a husband and wife went to their pastor and asked if they could take part in the marriage seminar coming up. The pastor said, "yes, but you must do something first." He said, "You must refrain from sex for this next week and we'll talk next Sunday." They agreed and off they went. Next Sunday came and the pastor met the couple and asked how it was going. "Well," the husband said, "it's been pretty hard but we made it." "OK," said the pastor, "now go another week without sex and we'll talk again next Sunday." The next Sunday arrived and the pastor asked again, how it was going. The husband replied, "We were doing great until Thursday." "What happened Thursday," the pastor asked. "My wife was in front of me and she bent over and I couldn't wait any longer, I took her right then." "Well," the pastor said, "you can't come to the seminar," "that's OK," replied the husband, "they won't allow us back in Food World anymore either.

Sexual responses of men and women are very different. I heard one speaker say that women respond like an electric stove. You push the button to turn on the burner and there's no immediate response. Slowly the burner warms up until its red-hot. When you turn the burner off, it continues to be red-hot and then slowly cools back down. Men, on the other hand, respond like a gas burner—instant on, instant off. Gary Smalley uses a similar metaphor. He says that women warm up like Crock-Pots, while men are like microwaves.

I believe sexuality must also be a gift. Simultaneous climax is wonderful, but giving the gift of understanding can bring its own form of joy to your relationship. Sacrificing to please your spouse sexually is a mature gift of love. Paul explains God's picture of true unity:

> *Do nothing out of selfish ambition or vain conceit, but in humility consider others better than yourselves. Each of you should look not only to your own interests, but also to the interest of others. Your attitude should be the same as that of Christ Jesus. (Phil 2:3-5)*

To be a gift, it has to be willingly given. The question most often asked is what is permissible and acceptable to God in the area of marital sexuality? Let's look at some scripture before we try and answer this question.

For this reason a man will leave his father and mother and be united to his wife, and they will become one flesh. (Gen 2:24)

Sex is between a man and his wife. No one else should be a participant – not in person, in print, or on video. That's why pornography is detrimental; it violates the prime directive of sexual love. Sex is between you two alone.

Marriage should be honored by all, and the marriage bed kept pure, for God will judge the adulterer and all the sexually immoral. (Heb 13:4)

Sex is designed for married couples. Any sexual activity outside marriage is like hot coals outside of a fireplace. In the right place it gives great pleasure and warmth but taken outside the place it was intended for will result in getting burned.

The husband should fulfill his marital duty to his wife, and likewise the wife to her husband. The wife's body does not belong to her alone but also to her husband. In the same way, the husband's body does not belong to him alone but also to his wife. Do not deprive each other except by mutual consent and for a time, so that you may devote yourselves to prayer. Then come together again so that Satan will

not tempt you because of your lack of self-control.
(1 Cor 7:3-5).

Marriage is designed to give sexual pleasure to each other. It is interesting that the Bible has very little to say about what is acceptable or unacceptable in the sexual expression of love between a husband and wife. Instead of a list of dos and don'ts the Bible presents guidelines:

1) Sexual love is to be given freely.
2) Every sexual activity is to be an expression of love.
3) Every intimate act is to be done with respect. This implies that you should only do what the two of you agree upon.

The Song of Solomon allows us to meet an insightful young groom who understands his wife's need and she his. To understand the passage, you must know that in the Song, the picture of a garden is used as a symbolic representation for a woman's vagina.

You are a garden locked up, my sister, my bride; you are a spring enclosed, a sealed fountain. Your plants are an orchard of pomegranates with choice fruits, with henna and nard, nard and saffron, calamus and cinnamon, with every kind of incense tree, with myrrh and aloes and all the finest spices. You are a garden fountain, a well of flowing water streaming down from Lebanon (SOS 4:12)

Notice that at the beginning of this scripture the garden is closed. But through the power of his words and caresses, the garden is flowing freely and fragrantly. Throughout the Song these two lovers experience encounters very similar to this, encouraging each of them to express their love.

The Song of Solomon can help us tremendously in our marriages especially with intimacy. I challenge you to let each other know what your desires are and to be willing to explore new horizons with your spouse.

SEX IS GOOD AND GOD MADE IT TO BE GOOD!!!

Here again are questions to help improve your love life. After answering them, commit to make the changes necessary to keep the fire burning in your marriage for a lifetime. As I stated in previous chapters it would be good to share your answers with your spouse.

1. How much time do I spend communicating with my spouse on a daily basis?

_____

_____

_____

2. In what ways can we improve our communication?

_____

_____

_____

3. How do I express love and what can I do to better show love to my spouse and family?

_____

_____

_____

4. In what ways can I increase the romance in my marriage?

_____

_____

_____

5. What can I do to improve our sex life?

_____

_____

_____

References

1. Zig Ziglar, "Courtship after Marriage," Zig Ziglar Corporation, 1994

2. Dietrick Bonhoeffer, "Wedding sermon for niece" http://joyma.com

3. Laura Moncur's Motivational Quotations, # 31121, www.quotationspage.com

4. Bernard Law Montgomery, "Memoirs of Field Marshall Montgomery," World Publishing Co. 1958

5. "The Seven Stumbling Blocks Ahead of Husbands," www.fountaingate.org/marital/rolefather.htm

6. Al Taylor, Proving God, Pathway, 1991.

7. US News and World Report, January, 1981

8. Houston, Texas Police Department, "How to Ruin Your Children,"

9. Dr. Paul D. Meier, "Christian Child-Rearing and Personality Development," Baker Book House. 1987

10. David Walters, "Children Aflame" Good New Fellowship Ministries. May 1995

11. Barna Research Group. 2003 results, www.barna.com

12. Gary Smalley, "Making Love Last Forever," Word Publishing. 1996

13. Lloyds of London, European Insurance Company Study

Recommended Reading

"Making Love Last Forever" by Gary Smalley

"Courtship After Marriage" by Zig Ziglar

"Christian Motivation for Daily Living" by Zig Ziglar

"Communication, key to your marriage" by H. Norman Wright

"Proving God" by Al Taylor

"Understanding Your Potential" by Dr. Myles Munroe

"The Language of Love" by Gary Smalley & John Trent, PhD

"Sexual Ethics, A Biblical Perspective" by Stanley Grenz

"Straight Talk to Men and Their Wives" by Dr. James Dobson

"When Good Men are Tempted" by Bill Perkins

"60 Things God Said About Sex" by Lester Sumrall

"Men Are Like Waffles Women Are Like Spaghetti" by Bill & Pam Farrel

"Strategies for a Successful Marriage" by E. Glenn Wagner, PhD

"The Five Love Languages" by Gary Chapman

"Tender Warrior "by Stu Weber

"Communication, Sex & Money" by Edwin Louis Cole

"Husbands & Fathers" by Derek Prince

"Love is a decision" by Gary Smalley & John Trent, Ph.D.

"Success by Design" by Dr. Peter Hirsch

The Author

Over thirty years ago this young man came to a Sunday morning church service, where I was attending at that time. Even though he didn't know what was happening Donny was being drawn by the Holy Spirit for the specific purpose of accepting Jesus Christ as his personal Savior. Although Donny's formative years were not spent in a Christian environment, there was never a lack of love and affection in his home. I fell in love with his kind, sweet, gentle, yet strong spirit and we were married in the fall of 1974. I love him more today than ever and he still makes me feel as though I am the most beautiful, desirable woman on the face of the earth. It makes me smile just to hear the sound of his voice on the other end of the telephone.

The desire of Donny's heart was always to be a husband and father. Even as a child Donny asked God for a wife and sons. God has blessed our marriage with three sons, two daughter-in-laws and two grandchildren. If I had searched the world over, I could have never found a man that would love me and his family more than Donny does. While the boys were growing up, he never failed to express both verbally and physically how much they were loved and appreciated. Therefore, they in turn are affectionate, tender young men sensitive to the direction of the Holy Spirit in their lives. Throughout our 30 years of marriage Donny's hunger for God and love of His Word has taught him how to be the extraordinary husband and father he has become. It is with conviction that I say Donny has truly walked out the pages of this book. To say that we have had a wonderful life without struggles and have never made mistakes would be a gross misrepresentation of the truth. There have been many days of anguish over the years, but through the mistakes God has developed character and wisdom in my husband. The anointing of God permeates his very being and has ignited his passion to help others discover the truths and promises in the Word of God.

This book has been many years in the making. It has finally emerged in an effort to help husbands, wives and families avoid some of the pitfalls and circumstances that could so easily overtake and destroy what God intended to be beautiful, long-lasting relationships. Our prayer is that this book will be a blessing to all who read it and apply the principles of the Word of God in their own lives.

Charlotte Ingram

Donny & Charlotte Ingram

They can be contacted by email at:
arkministry@aol.com
or by mail at
P.O. Box 1257
Oneonta, Alabama 35121

Information on training programs available to
corporations and organizations can be found at
Ingram Management Group web site:
www.ingrammanagement.com